MW01257490

SOULinks

Pursuing Multi-Generational Significance

Paulette
Wishing you much
Joy in your SOULinks
relationships
Warmly
Joan

Joan O. Wright

Library of Congress Control Number (LCCN): 2015920060
ISBN: 978-0-9825505-4-0

First Edition, February 2016

Published by:

JOW Publishing
Charlotte, North Carolina
www.osullivanwright.com

Front Cover Photo: Courtesy of Charlotte Observer Newspaper
Photographer: Gary O'Brien

Back Cover Photo: Courtesy of Deborah Triplett

Printed in the United States of America

SOULinks

Pursuing
Multi-Generational
Significance

Paulette
Wishing you much
Joy in your SOULinks
relationships
Warmly
Joan

Joan O. Wright

Library of Congress Control Number (LCCN): 2015920060
ISBN: 978-0-9825505-4-0

First Edition, February 2016

Published by:

JOW Publishing
Charlotte, North Carolina
www.osullivanwright.com

Front Cover Photo: Courtesy of Charlotte Observer Newspaper
Photographer: Gary O'Brien

Back Cover Photo: Courtesy of Deborah Triplett

Printed in the United States of America

To my beloved Mot.

Thanks for choosing to love me everyday.

To my beloved Mot.

Thanks for choosing to love me everyday.

Table of Contents

Extras

Preface

Life is a series of connections and relationships of all shapes, sizes and contexts. Some are desired, some are not. Some are intentional, others are surprises. Some are family, but most extend beyond blood boundaries. And some extend beyond peer and generational bounds. These are the relationships that have captured my attention, and my heart, for a number of reasons.

There are many very academic sounding terms for these relationships that leap across generations. We could call them multi-generational, cross-generational or inter-generational, and all play a role in the study of something we call intergenerationality and human geography. And, being the master label applicators we are, we have given these different generations names and assigned characteristics. We might differ a bit in descriptions and age ranges, but typically we understand the categories. You've heard names like "The Lost Generation," "The Greatest Generation" *(a term coined by Tom Brokaw),* "The Silent Generation," Baby Boomers, Gen X-ers, Gen-Y's, and Millennials.

For thousands of years we have relied upon the wisdom and experiences of those generations that came before us to enrich our own wisdom and knowledge. But lately the cross-generational relationship has been placed on the list of "endangered species." There are a number of reasons for this, including the fragility of today's family structures *(divorce, ease of travel and separation, etc.),* cultural and values differences *(to one generation LBJ is Lyndon Baines*

Johnson; to the other, it is LeBron James), and, perhaps the biggest generational gap generator, technology *(the generation with ancient VCRs that still blink 12:00, versus the globally connected who are masters at social media and all things digital).*

Not only has technology caused a generational gap that widens exponentially faster than the click of a mouse, it has also developed a *social relationship* gap that is troubling. We seem to be losing our ability to communicate face-to-face, develop social skills, and promote personal relationships. Now it's all done with our fingertips, separated, remote and distant. Personal relationships are moving over in favor of digital – and impersonal – relationships. I read an article recently that made the bold statement *(I'm paraphrasing and summarizing)* that we are the most affluent society ever, yet we are also the most depressed, isolated and addicted society ever. Wow. That should tell us something needs our attention – fast.

Studies have shown that today's "elder" generation is more depressed and isolated than at any other time in history. They believe they have become "irrelevant" and unneeded. And today's young adults are also depressed and disheartened more than ever, because they are fearful about their futures and haven't lived enough life to see there are ways through these hard times. The solution to this situation seems obvious, doesn't it?

I read a quote that made such beautiful sense to me, and should become our "mantra" for the promotion of multi-generational relationships: *"My younger friends connect me to where I've been, and my older friends connect me to where I'm going."*[1] The older population feels irrelevant because they believe they've outlived their usefulness – they have lived too long. The younger adult generation hasn't lived long enough to help them successfully navigate into their future. The "what has been's" and the "what can be's" provide the missing ingredients for both generations when they team up. The younger generation helps connect the older to their past (validating all the knowledge and wisdom they have acquired), while the older generation helps pave the way and reveal insights about building a future for their younger friends. Talk about mutually beneficial. Depression, sadness, and despair were shared by *both* generations, but can be *banished* for both when the two generations meet up. It is like a beautiful, logical mathematical equation. It makes perfect sense.

Generations can feel distant and unconnected because of technological advancement. Yes, technology is wonderful, but there is a price to pay unless we actively seek to overcome its negative side. For me, that activism is seeking and establishing fruitful, mutually beneficial, mutually needed multi-generational relationships. We may not be able to link up at the technology level, but we can and should link at the *soul* level. The wisdom and experience we need cannot always be found at the click of that mouse or tap of a tiny keypad. Hence, SOULinks.

I am particularly passionate about this subject because I have lived and experienced it in my own family and my network of friends and colleagues. The first story you will read is about our son, Andrew. Andrew would not be the very vibrant successful professional he is today without one particular cross-generational relationship. That is no exaggeration, but I will let his story speak for itself. The stories contained here are all familiar to me. Some are my own stories and some belong to my friends and professional connections. All of them have been chosen to inspire, to get you thinking, seeking and reaching out.

I would like to challenge you the reader – young or old – to pursue significance by reaching out across generations, regardless of the presence *(or lack)* of a "blood" connection *(family)* to seek and embrace multi-generational relationships wherever you can find them. The mutual benefits are surprising and welcome, adding a layer of richness to our lives that nothing else can.

This book is intended to touch your heart first, then as a call to engagement and action. We need each other still, regardless of technology, cultural or age differences. Where will you find your multi-generational relationships? How will you nurture them? I hope this book helps answer some of your questions, but more than that, I hope it moves you to action.

Joan O. Wright, MSW, MCC
February 2016

> What love we've given, we'll have forever.
> What love we fail to give, will be lost for all eternity.
> —*Leo Buscaglia*

[1] Theresa Carey, in "The Value of Intergenerational Relationships" by Joseph Hart, *Experience Life magazine*, July/August 2012, https://experiencelife.com/article/the-value-of-intergenerational-relationships/)

SOULinks

Chapter

Jennie and Andrew

The Inn at Little Washington is truly beyond description. People seem to lack words enough to adequately praise this glamorous lodging and world famous restaurant nestled in the countryside of Virginia, named after our first President who founded and surveyed this town in 1769. This picturesque place is a delightful step into the past, a time when concrete and superhighways were beyond imagination. And the food – well, the food is incredible. Chef and Proprietor Patrick O'Connell, is often described as "The Pope of American Cuisine," and his restaurant attracts people from around the world. Some have said that the food here is so good it "makes you cry."

This is where Andrew currently practices his passion. He is the executive sous chef in this auspicious place. But Andrew's beginnings were far less auspicious, and his journey to reach this place is one filled with remarkable relationships and seemingly divine direction.

He was born in Atlanta and given up for adoption a mere 48 hours after his birth. The doctor who delivered him placed him in the arms of his new parents at a park near the hospital where he was born. Shortly before this day, Andrew's new Dad had taken a job in Charlotte, North Carolina. He was building his career as an architect, and returning to his home town he had left some 20 years before. As soon as the State of Georgia cleared it, Andrew's new family moved back to North Carolina, into the Myers Park neighborhood, a few months after his birth.

Myers Park is a beautiful suburb of Charlotte. The natural curves, gentle hills and creeks create a secluded, pastoral area removed from the bustling city nearby. Beautiful tree-lined streets with very generous front and back yards made the perfect place to raise a family. Mature willow and pin oak trees shade and protect the yards in the heat of the summer. Today Myers Park is a prestigious address. Back then, when Andrew and his family moved there, it was an older neighborhood "re-gentrifying" with younger couples. It had been a neighborhood of mostly older residents, with a few urban singles scattered about. As more young families moved in, the mix of old and young offered the perfect atmosphere for generation-spanning friendships and multi-generational mentoring. It was a neighborhood whose residents, one in particular, would shape Andrew's future and his passion.

Tom and Jennie lived next door to Andrew's family. They were in their mid-60's at this time, both recently retired. Tom was a general practitioner with a servant's heart, choosing to serve the poorer side of Charlotte, often seeing dozens of patients each day. Jennie managed Tom's busy practice for many years, and shared his heart for people. Jennie and Tom were ready for their roles as grandparents when Andrew conveniently moved in next door. He was just a few months old, but Jennie fell in love with him at first sight. Both families connected immediately. Jennie was warm and welcoming and Tom was witty, proud of his "curmudgeon" name tag. This was home, and this was family.

The kitchen is often called the "heart of the home." Yet both of these kitchens had something missing –

Both of Andrew's paternal grandparents had passed away before his father moved the family back to Charlotte, and Tom and Jennie's kids were not local so they didn't have regular contact with them or their grandchildren. With both houses having back doors that opened directly into the kitchen only 25 feet apart, you couldn't set up a better opportunity for a beautiful relationship.

In her retirement, Jennie loved to cook. The kitchen is often called the "heart of the home." Yet both of these kitchens had something missing – one lacked little ones underfoot, the other the wisdom and love only a grandparent can offer. But this lack was not long-lived. As far as Andrew was concerned, there were no boundaries between these two homes. He "owned" and lived in both. Tom and Jennie were his family. Separated by only a happy run, skip and hop on short eager legs for both regular and impromptu visits, both kitchens were now complete.

Andrew would literally run next door, and pop into Jennie's kitchen where she was always preparing something wonderful. She was a great cook, and a great and patient teacher. Andrew was by her side all the time, and Jennie taught him all the basics of cooking. Not only did Andrew love to help prepare Jennie's food, he also loved to eat it. When he was two years old he called her broccoli "trees." Andrew's entire family would often eat next door, as Tom performed his own magic with his charcoal grill. Andrew delighted in watching his granddaddy start the fire with a single sheet of newspaper.

Every Thanksgiving and Christmas Andrew's family was invited to join their celebrations. They were all one big family. Andrew, and later his sister Emma Kate, would play in both family yards. Tom and Jennie were home most of the time, and the kids had the run of both properties. It was a safe, warm wonderland for both Andrew and Emma Kate.

While both Tom and Jennie were grandpa and grandma to Andrew, his real SOULink was Jennie. Andrew grew up in Jennie's kitchen, becoming her very own executive sous chef. Little did anyone guess that the kitchen would one day become Andrew's castle, the place where he would ultimately fulfill his passion and purpose.

Unfortunately, this ideal cross-generational relationship suffered a bit of a bump in the road as Andrew's parents' marriage was rocky, and soon a divorce was looming. Everyone felt the strain, especially Andrew. He had learned that a good meal has great power to bring people together, and in his young mind all it would take is a great dinner and things would be fine. At the age of six Andrew prepared a very special meal with his grandmother's help to ease the building tensions. Unfortunately the divide in his family could not be fixed by a lovely meal lovingly prepared by young hands with a big heart.

Andrew also had learning disabilities and attended special schools, but things were tough for him there. With growing tensions at home and difficulties in school, Andrew often spent his "alone" time, not alone, but with his loving grandparents who were always there during Andrew's emotional ups and downs. In these moments in grandma's kitchen Andrew developed a love of cooking. It became his joy, and would provide focus and help keep him centered amidst growing turmoil.

It is also important to understand that this relationship of cook and protégé was not one-sided. Jennie had her share of tough times, too. Having Andrew in her life made a huge difference, and offered Jennie the joy of being needed and unconditionally loved at times when she didn't experience that in other places. When the anxiety and tension at home were too much for Andrew he would walk next door to escape, and in doing this, he also provided Jennie an escape from her own troubles. Together they had created a loving and mutually beneficial bond for life.

Even while living through difficult times, both of Andrew's parents were welcomed in Tom and Jennie's home. And when the divorce finally came, the bond that had been developed over the first six years of Andrew's life was firmly in place and could not be broken, despite the fact that Andrew's family moved away. Andrew divided his time between both parents for a year, but his mom really wanted a daughter and never developed a strong bond with Andrew. When his mom's second marriage broke up, Andrew went to live with his dad. Although their kitchens were not mere feet away any more, Andrew's and Jennie's hearts were still joined. When Andrew's Dad had both children, they would all hang out with Tom and Jennie. Andrew's Dad says they provided him much needed love, counsel, stability and comfort during those years. Tom and Jennie would travel frequently just to attend the kids' various recitals, ballgames and other childhood activities. The relationship with Jennie and Andrew grew stronger, as did Andrew's culinary skills.

The relationship with Jennie and Andrew grew stronger, as did Andrew's culinary skills.

Jennie would often take Andrew shopping with her at the local grocery, a small somewhat gourmet neighborhood store where you could sign a tab for whatever you purchased. Jennie taught Andrew every facet of cooking, including the importance of buying the proper ingredients. Later, when Andrew was 15, he worked here as a bagger and checkout clerk. He already had a long history with this store, always at Jennie's side. They made him feel special. Much later, when Andrew was at Johnson & Wales University College of Culinary Arts, he befriended the wine supplier who encouraged him to shoot for the moon and apply to the French Laundry in Napa, California, recognized as one of the world's finest restaurants. He did, and he was accepted, working there two years as *Chef de partie*. This opportunity would not have happened if Andrew's grandmother Jennie had not initiated the relationships and opened doors for Andrew.

Even well after the divorce of Andrew's parents, Tom and Jennie continued in the grandparent relationship. Family ties had been well established and a few miles could not separate them. Andrew and his Dad lived together for about five years when a new woman entered this bachelor pad culture. Three years later, this gal who grew up with only a sister and went to an all-girls school was now Andrew's new mom. It took some time and major adjustments for her to adapt to this completely foreign guys-only lifestyle. The relationship between Andrew, his Dad and Jennie and Tom was so firmly in place that Andrew's new mom considered Jennie her mother-in-law.

In his teens Andrew worked in the food industry, deciding to pursue what had become his passion. After graduation from Johnson & Wales, and working in many world class restaurants, today Andrew is living his dream as the executive sous chef at the Inn at Little Washington. This dream was born in the kitchen next door many years before. Listen to what Andrew has written on his resume, regarding his personal philosophy and cooking:

> *Cooking is so much more than just a job. It's a life.*
>
> *This life provides me opportunities every day to do what I love – to coach, mentor, teach, and lead. I learned these values from my grandmother, in her kitchen, when I was three years old. As a result, I think of her every time I make not only a specific sauce, but also a connection with a new team member.*

> *Cooking is as much about the people and relationships as it is about the art and craft. I believe in creating an exceptional culinary experience fueled by great coaching. I give my team the culinary training and mentoring that I learned at a young age, so that they each may be better in the kitchen today, but also go further in their careers.*
>
> *In coaching team members well in the kitchen, we give those whom we serve an unforgettable experience fueled by focus, clarity, communication, and the heart of a high-performing team that drives the profitable growth of a restaurant* or concept.
>
> *This life provides so much more than just a meal.*

It's easy to see that not only did Jennie help Andrew craft and develop his passion in life and go on to excel as a master in culinary arts, but she also passed along her ability and desire to mentor others. Jennie is gone now, but Andrew is living out her legacy, and it all started in a seemingly simple kitchen-based cross-generational relationship that filled so many needs. This is truly an amazing journey that began with visits to the "grandma" next door, by a boy who was diagnosed and labeled dyslexic, one whom the "experts" said would never go to college. If they could only see him now. It didn't take experts. It took a loving grandmother.

One more thing. Just as Jennie was Andrew's true grandmother, Andrew is my true son. And I couldn't be prouder. Don't worry, I managed to whip those guys living the bachelor life into shape, loving every minute of it. And loving Andrew and Jennie in the process.

Chapter

You and Me

In chapter one you read about the remarkable journey of my son Andrew, given direction and passion by a most amazing multi-generational relationship with his next-door grandma, Jennie. Andrew went from a toddler watching Jennie cook in her kitchen to being an executive sous chef in one of the most prestigious restaurants in the world. There is no doubt in my mind that this relationship was critical in guiding Andrew into discovering and living his dream.

Now I want to speak to you directly, to give you a little bit more about this subject, what has driven me to write this book, and what I hope will inspire you to pursue significance through multi-generational relationships.

I have always had a passion about mentoring relationships, and have featured many of these in my book *UP: Pursuing Significance in Leadership and Life.*[2] Whether in professional or personal application, I know that mentoring is one of the most productive and satisfying pursuits, and I often promote these kinds of relationships in my work as an executive coach with high level business leaders. I am also aware of the beautiful fruit harvested from these mentoring relationships in our personal lives. So my ears immediately perked up as I watched the *Today Show* one day and listened to a researcher talk about her latest project involving depression.[3]

Dr. Sara M. Moorman, an assistant professor in the Department of Sociology and the Institute on Aging at Boston College said *"We found that an emotionally close grandparent-adult grandchild relationship was associated with fewer symptoms of depression for both generations... The greater emotional support grandparents and adult grandchildren received from one another, the better their psychological health."*[4] This was a watershed moment for me. I have spent my entire career coaching people to find and pursue their passions, and then, as leaders, to share their experiences with others. I sat there a bit amazed, having just had a glimpse of my newest calling – "SOULinks," the book you hold in your hands right now.

We all know the benefits of a close and loving relationship between grandparents and their young grandchildren. What we often overlook, however, is the incredible richness and significance of these multi-generational relationships among *adult* grandchildren. I listened more attentively to Dr. Moorman who shared that the research also revealed that when grandparents receive, but do not give to such a relationship, they are much more likely to experience depression. When they can give, as well as receive, benefits to their grandchildren, depression in the older generation *decreases* markedly. For both the adult grandchild and the grandparents to be less depressed, both parties in this relationship must give and take mutually.

The study concluded that by encouraging more grand-parents and adult grandchildren to engage in this give and take exchange, it would result in dramatically lowering the chances of depression among older adults, as well as the adult grandchild. To fully reap all the benefits of multi-generational relationships, however, the give and take must consist of more than special gifts or one-time giving to an adult grandchild. Giving tangible things is only a small part of such a relationship. When the grandparent can provide experience, guidance, wisdom, emotional support and unconditional love, the mutually beneficial results soar. I personally experienced this through Andrew and Jennie's relationship, well into Andrew's adult years.

This mentoring relationship can exist and function just as well outside the typical family boundaries. Studies have shown remarkable results even among non-family, or extended family, multi-generational relationships – just like the one Andrew had with Jennie. When older people believe they are providing benefits to the younger generation, they feel more productive, useful, and needed. When the adult "grandchild" receives the benefit of an elder's life experiences they are receiving caring support that can often help them navigate through some of life's more difficult lessons.

The uniqueness of the adult grandchild-grandparent relationship is due largely to parents who have to walk a tightrope between mercy and tough love, as well as professional and personal obligations. The grandparent is not restricted in these ways. He or she can offer unconditional mercy, love, support and caring despite the mistakes made by the "grandchild." Grandparents usually have plenty of time, and have already pursued their professional goals. They are beyond the need to keep climbing the ladder, so to speak. Parents of young adults are typically still engaged in their professional pursuits, and lack the time and even patience to deal with all the emotional needs of children who are "supposed to be on their own by now." But grandparents are beyond that, and we all know that being needed is a vital and critical human need. By the time retirement has come, and professional challenges are over, the retiree often feels unneeded, or that what they have achieved means little without someone to share it with. Adult grandchildren often don't understand what they need, or where to get what they need.

Dr. Stephen Covey promoted a model with three life stages of dependence, independence and inter-dependence. Today we promote and encourage our young people to become independent, but we sorely neglect the all-important final stage of *inter*-dependence. Interdependence is the place where we team up with others for greater goals and outcomes than mere independence can bring. Instead, we tend to exalt independence, finally growing into that place where we stand alone, needing no one. What a lonely, unproductive and unfulfilled place that is. Multi-generational relationships are the epitome of interdependence, providing richness for both parties, and vital nourishment for the growing of future generations.

As I researched the significance of multi-generational relationships, I came across a most startling and troubling study. The Huffington Post headlined an article titled *"Google Replacing Grandparents? Bleak New Study Says 'Yes.'"*[5] This article spoke of a study conducted by an unlikely source, a British manufacturer of cleaning products, "Dr. Beckmann®." The study consisted of 1500 British grandparents who were asked if they had been approached for advice about domestic things like sewing, family recipes, even laundry tips. Apparently only one in five grandparents said "yes." In generations past, grandparents were the ones who filled in the gaps about everyday life lessons like these, but no longer. The study researchers found that adult grandchildren were seeking the answers to their questions by going to the Internet instead. Those grandparents surveyed felt like their roles as experienced advice-givers to the younger generation were becoming obsolete. They were no longer needed. Today's generation of young people no longer rely on the trusted and time-valued experiences of their elders. They simply "Google" what they need. Without the perception of being needed, or being relevant, depression is not far behind.

We can change this. We *must* change this. While technology is often a huge benefit to mankind, it has likely stripped us of tapping the incredibly rich resource of the older generation's life experiences, unconditional love and emotional support. It has also contributed to the rise of depression among our elders, and the decrease in embracing caring relationships available to our young adult population. This trend is increasing, but so will my efforts to change it.

In our materialistic culture, another valuable asset lost when multi-generational relationships falter is the incredible richness of traditional values. Some have said that our current "younger" generation has *no* values, except materialism, entitlement and self-centeredness. How did that happen? While this is certainly not true of every young adult, it is prevalent today partly because we have not passed them along from generation to generation. In the past, this was a vital role of the grandparent.

I have long admired the traditionally Jewish practice of something called a "Jewish Will" or an "ethical will." These documents have their ancient roots in Judaism, but regardless of belief or faith, it is a mindset and a valuable tradition we all need to insure a more values-based future. An Ethical, or Jewish Will, is a written document that is designed to allow a person to pass on their ethical and moral values from one generation to the next. It has become more and more popular with the general public in the past few decades, but the Jews have been doing this for millennia. Its origins are apparently in the book of Genesis, when Jacob was dying and blessed his sons.[6] It is seen in Moses' speeches to the people of Israel before he died, and many other occasions in the Jewish scriptures (the Old Testament, or Hebrew Tanakh). This practice of passing on belief systems and values, dreams and goals, became a Jewish tradition which today is even used among the general public for estate planning.

Some of these ethical wills are beautiful pieces of poetic and emotional language meant also to convey the person's great love, and treasured values, to the ones left behind. In this case the valuables left to loved ones are the *values* themselves. Sadly, this practice of elders passing on their values is missing in most families, one of the victims of decreasing multi-generational relationships.

Our world cries out for these long-term, loving and lasting relationships among generations. We have become isolated, small worlds to ourselves, even though we have global reach. We spend too much time communicating via technology, and becoming compartmentalized instead of promoting relationships. We drive up our driveways and shut the doors. Our young people are facing a scary world without the benefit of an older generation's experiences, wisdom, values and loving support that can help them successfully navigate this often terrifying place we all live.

In 2004 our local newspaper *The Charlotte Observer,* ran an article which began *"Years ago, a young boy's next door neighbor invited him to watch her in the kitchen. Now he could be the city's most promising young chef."* This article told readers about an unlikely friendship that lasted over 20 years, and the glue that bonded them was a love of cooking. Jennie knew how to transfer her love of cooking into a mentoring relationship with this young boy who, because of her wisdom and influence, dreamed of being a world class chef. Andrew dreamed it, and he became it.

As for me and my house, we have taken first steps, sometimes baby steps, to reunite our children with their grandparents, and even with those who are no longer here, but contributed to their own uniqueness. Personally, I am committed to making this cause one that I will incorporate as an integrated part of my work, and my immediate and extended family and personal relationships. I am calling this "SOULinks" because these interactions are truly bonds made at the soul level in multi-generational relationships. We owe it to our children, our elders, and to our future generations to make every effort to re-establish the vibrancy and significance of multi-generational relationships.

I have told you what I will do, and the importance of these significant multi-generational relationships. *What will you do?* The stories that follow here are short, easy to read real-life examples of multi-generational relationships. My intent with this book is not to cover this subject academically, but to move you to action – to inspire you to seek your own significance in this area.

Read on...your SOULink is out there.

Chapter *Three*

Isabelle and Meg

Meg met Isabelle when she was three years old, after her family moved to Long Island, New York from Philadelphia. Isabelle and her husband lived next door. Meg doesn't recall the first time she saw Isabelle, but thinks it was probably with her mom shortly after they moved there. The houses here were very close together, and the neighborhood very safe and friendly. It was quite natural for Meg to run next door, ring the bell and spend hours with Isabelle. Meg's own grandparents were not nearby in this new and different place. In their 50's and retired, Isabelle and her husband had two grown children of their own who were right out of college and working their first jobs, but had not yet started families of their own. Isabelle once told Meg that she was her first grandchild, one who had an invitation to just walk in, anytime.

Meg remembers that the time she spent with Isabelle was never about princesses and dolls. It wasn't even playing games. The time they spent together was in serious talk about life – as much life as any three-year-old might know. Even from that early age, however, Meg was interested in more than mere play. She had a love for books and reading, and the adventure of learning new things, new perspectives and new possibilities. Isabelle had this grand floor-to-ceiling bookcase that beckoned Meg, who would choose any book she liked, and she and Isabelle would read together and discuss what was read. Isabelle was a former New York City school teacher who knew kids and how to discover their potential. Isabelle encouraged Meg's reading and literary adventures, including storytelling. At one point she told Meg's mother that Meg would become a writer, and her sister would likely be an actress. Incredibly, she was right on both counts.

At one point she told Meg's mother that Meg would become a writer, and her sister would likely be an actress. Incredibly, she was right on both counts.

Besides the excitement of books at Isabelle's house there was also the most amazing collection of original artwork. Together Meg and Isabelle would look carefully at each piece and talk about the artist and what he or she had produced from their imagination and skill. They would talk for hours. Isabelle was Meg's pal, confidante and mentor. And along the way, through hours of contented talks together, Meg's world was being broadened in a way nothing else could compare.

Isabelle and her husband were Armenian, and Meg also learned about cultural differences. Meg's family was invited to share in their church life during Easter, Christmas, Palm

Sunday and other religious holidays. Meg learned that people had traditions that were a little bit different from her suburban Protestant upbringing. She experienced a rich expansiveness around religion, culture, hospitality and values through Isabelle.

Meg admits she was a precocious child. In fact, she says she got in trouble in Kindergarten for speaking her mind *(something you are apparently not supposed to do at that age)*, but she learned that sense of self from Isabelle, a native New Yorker, Armenian by heritage, mother, teacher, and well-educated woman who knew exactly who she was. When Meg sometimes jokes about this sense of self, displayed sometimes with what she calls "sass and attitude," she is convinced she got it from Isabelle, her first and lifelong SOULink.

Being right next door and having parents who promoted this relationship facilitated this bond between Meg and Isabelle. But Meg's family moved away a few years later and the daily contact with Isabelle was broken, yet soul bonds continued. Meg and Isabelle have kept in touch for almost 30 years, including some visits. Now Isabelle is in her late 80s and time has taken its toll. She is no longer able to communicate quite as well, and sometimes has to be encouraged to even remember who Meg is, but once the pieces come together Isabelle remembers everything and brightens instantly. For Meg it is very hard to see this connection slowly slip away, due solely to age. Life paths merged for Meg's formative years, and Isabelle left an indelible mark on a little girl, while seeing her own natural mentor's heart fulfilled.

In her 20s and fresh out of college, one of Meg's first jobs was teaching the 12th grade. She remembers how Isabelle's desire to mentor influenced Meg and her students. Even today Meg hears more from her previous students who have now gone onto their own families and careers than even her former colleagues in the professional world. Isabelle threw a pebble into a receptive pond, and the ripples are still widening.

Today Meg is indeed a successful writer who has contributed both in the creative and the technical genres. In addition to writing a column for the Huffington Post *(among other writing ventures)*, she is on her fifth children's book. Meg has an MBA, and has worked in the corporate arena, but her passion is –*one guess*–mentoring, especially young people. Her children's book series reflects both Isabelle's early influence, and Meg's own interests. Titled *"Bea is for Business,"* this children's series is designed to teach kids all about business. Meg is building cross-generational relationships into her books by including an older character who mentors children – one who looks, talks and acts remarkably like Isabelle. In addition to her passion for writing, Meg also has a passion for art, another love instilled by Isabelle.

Because of her extraordinary SOULink with Isabelle at an early age, when she was forming her own personality, goals and passions, Meg believes that everyone needs to realize these relationships can exist anywhere, and encourage them. Within families they are wonderful, but there is a lot of power in connecting with someone not in your immediate family. A neighbor or a friend can expose you to things you would never experience within family boundaries. Isabelle established a passion and pattern for Meg's life. Isabelle knew that nurturing, mentoring and passing on what you know and who you are can make all the difference in both lives. In many respects it is how we move gracefully into the future, and how legacies live beyond us.

Could your SOULink be right next door?

We make a living by what we get,
but we make a life by what we give.

Winston Churchill

Chapter

Mrs. Sparkle and Carol

There are potential *grand*parents and *grand*kids all around you, everywhere you look. All we have to do is slow down a little bit and take the time to observe the people around us. They may be in your own family, or they may be just next door, down the street, at the grocery store, or in places you would never have imagined. Just keep watching.

During the summer one year Carol's family rented a vacation home in a seaside summer resort town in New England. This tiny town has a population of just a few hundred most of the year, but swells to thousands during peak summer weekends. This particular year Carol and her husband and four young boys rented a home from Mrs. Sparkle. This was the first time Mrs. Sparkle rented her home, one of the nicest on the island, and had never met Carol or her family. All of their correspondence was through a real estate agent. Carol is only guessing, but she's pretty sure Mrs. Sparkle had not thought a young family with four boys under the age of six, including one squirming crawling baby, was probably the ideal tenant for her beautiful home.

Carol remembers hearing how important it was for her to keep Mrs. Sparkle's home nice and clean. Mrs. Sparkle had a cleaning lady, part of the rental package, to come do all those things for Carol and "her little darlings," as Carol puts it. The cleaning lady told Carol that Mrs. Sparkle was a bit upset to discover that her renters were a family with four small boys. Upon hearing this somewhat disturbing news, the cleaning lady told Carol that she and Mrs. Sparkle embarked on a thorough campaign to remove her valuable and breakable stuff to the protective off limits of the basement. Carol and family spent a month in Mrs. Sparkle's lovely home. Carol thought she had done everything well, according to Mrs. Sparkle's directions. That is, until their last day.

On the last morning of their time in Mrs. Sparkle's home, Carol sent her husband out of the house with the boys, and cleaned that home better than she had cleaned anything her entire life. Satisfied that Mrs. Sparkle would appreciate her efforts, the family headed to the car to leave by noon, as their contract specified. On an impulsive whim, her oldest son ran back to "say goodbye to the house." Running back out, he managed to put his entire hand through the screen on the front door. But it was time to leave. Carol couldn't do anything about the screen. She imagined Mrs. Sparkle later pulling up to her lovely house and seeing her screen door sporting a new gaping hole.

Carol and her family ended up renting a different house the following year. She had not yet met Mrs. Sparkle, and didn't know just how "cool" she was. Carol thought a house closer to the beach, one more "lived in" was appropriate for her family with four young boys. That next summer Carol and Mrs. Sparkle were finally introduced at cocktails before dinner at the local beach club. Within minutes they were fully engaged in an entertaining and fun conversation. Throughout the course of the summer Carol and Mrs. Sparkle kept finding themselves in the same places at the same time – places like the grocery store and the post office. Perhaps the universe was conspiring to make them friends.

Even though she and her family rented a different house that year, Carol loved Mrs. Sparkle's home and remembered some of the innovative things Mrs. Sparkle had incorporated, even adopting many of them in her next renovation project. Things like proper little drawers for all the DVDs, and her favorite, a square box where she kept printed cocktail napkins with the funniest and sometimes most irreverent sayings. She fondly recalls going through the box of napkins and howling in laughter. She remembers a few sayings right off the top of her head, like *"Marriage is like a deck of cards. In the beginning it's all hearts and diamonds, but in the end you wish you had clubs and spades – to club them and then bury them!"* Or the one that read, *"Wedding dress for sale. Worn once by mistake."* One day, at one of their unplanned encounters, Carol asked Mrs. Sparkle about them. And with this collection of funny cocktail napkins began one of the dearest relationships Carol treasures.

And with this collection of funny cocktail napkins began one of the dearest relationships Carol treasures.

Since their initial return from renting Mrs. Sparkle's house that summer, Carol kept a look out for funny cocktail napkins, collected and then sent them to Mrs. Sparkle, who started doing the same thing, sending them to Carol. Trading cocktail napkins progressed to trading funny cards and other humorous items. Carol found a kindred soul in Mrs. Sparkle's humor. This relationship continued in this manner for years, with Carol and Mrs. Sparkle seeing each other only a few times during the summer when they were vacationing *(not in Mrs. Sparkle's house!).*

A few years ago Carol and her husband actually bought their own house in Mrs. Sparkle's beloved seaside town. As soon as Carol was there, Mrs. Sparkle kindly came over to help rearrange the hodgepodge of furniture that came with the house, even loaning some of her "basement treasures." She was well into her 70's, but started throwing down dish towels on the floor *(apparently the early version of those plastic coasters used to move furniture)* so they could move things easily. Mrs. Sparkle isn't a couch vegetable. This woman is actively involved in her own daughters' lives, and the lives of all those around her. She is busy and vital, and always with that gleam of mischievous humor that appeals so much to Carol's own slightly irreverent side.

Carol began renovating their vacation house, with Mrs. Sparkle right there huddled over the blueprints with her. They love having double dates and lots of laughter over an occasional cup of tea together. And even though their laughter should have made them fear being thrown out of a few of the more respectable establishments in this town, they never minded the stares. Let the world see their joy. Although Mrs. Sparkle is from an "older generation," this woman still has a spark that ignites and sustains her relationship with Carol. Carol helps Mrs. Sparkle conquer those huge technical challenges like how to send a picture on your iPhone. Mrs. Sparkle may be the "mature" generation (as some are now politely calling them), but she wants to live in the present, not the past. Carol says it is Mrs. Sparkle's humor and zest for living today that is like a magnet to her and others.

Other than about a month in the summers, this relationship is long distance, but joined in a timeless way by funny cocktail napkins and a *commitment to be in relationship.* Mrs. Sparkle is like everyone's favorite grandmother. Carol remembers one year when her oldest son *(the same one who put his hand through Mrs. Sparkle's screen door many years earlier)*, thirteen years old at the time, was driving her crazy and she said so to Mrs. Sparkle. Mrs. Sparkle responded by telling Carol to send him to her, she would put him to work. That she did, hiring him and keeping him busy helping with their sailboats and other summer activities that 80-year olds aren't able to do on their own any longer. Mrs. Sparkle calls him her "swabbie." She has an innate sense of people, what they need, and how to connect. To Carol, she is truly a treasure. Mrs. Sparkle has reached the age where frenetic activity is not the norm. This generation is more laid back, enjoying every day for what it holds. Things don't always have to happen "right now." Carol says it's a wonderful gift to have that kind of influence in her life. It balances and evens out the craziness of younger generations in today's world.

Carol says, *"When I'm with Mrs. Sparkle I feel I can naturally be more of who I really am - more of myself."* Parent-child relationships can tend to be a little judgmental, and as they age together in the relationship they are more inclined to be guarded around parents and even when reaching adulthood, children are always *ingrained and imagined as children* by their parents. Children can feel if they say or do certain things around their parents, they are asking for a lecture or judgment. We all need those safe places where we can just be ourselves and know there is acceptance, a listening ear, and not immediate judgment or censorship. Carol is always relaxed with Mrs. Sparkle, with no need or sense of having to be guarded. The mental health benefits from this kind of relationship are better than any anti-depressant or gin and tonic. These relationships cut through stress like butter, leaving only a melted puddle of warmth where anxiety, tension, and perhaps even parental expectations, had formerly "hardened our arteries." Expectations can shut up hearts tight like impenetrable fortresses. Freedom to *be* opens the doors wide. Carol loves the exuberance, new energy and different perspectives that come from this mutually satisfying multi-generational relationship.

And these wonderful connections can begin right under our noses, in the least expected places, if we only pay attention. They can even begin with broken screen doors and funny cocktail napkins in a little seaside resort.

Chapter

Harry Chapin and Bob

Harry Chapin, of course, was the singer-songwriter who composed (with his wife Sandy) and sang the popular song "Cat's in the Cradle," which skyrocketed to the top of the charts in 1974. The lyrics are sobering, and just about everyone could *(and still can)* relate to them in one way or the other.

My child arrived just the other day
He came to the world in the usual way
But there were planes to catch, and bills to pay
He learned to walk while I was away
And he was talking 'fore I knew it, and as he grew
He'd say, "I'm gonna be like you, dad
You know I'm gonna be like you."

[Chorus]
And the cat's in the cradle and the silver spoon
Little boy blue and the man in the moon
"When you coming home, dad?" "I don't know when
But we'll get together then
You know we'll have a good time then."

My son turned ten just the other day
He said, "Thanks for the ball, dad; come on, let's play
Can you teach me to throw?"
I said, "Not today, I got a lot to do."
He said, "That's okay."
And he walked away, but his smile never dimmed
And said, "I'm gonna be like him, yeah
You know I'm gonna be like him."

[Chorus]

Well, he came from college just the other day
So much like a man, I just had to say
"Son, I'm proud of you. Can you sit for a while?"
He shook his head, and he said with a smile
"What I'd really like, dad, is to borrow the car keys
See you later; can I have them please?"
And the cat's in the cradle and the silver spoon
Little boy blue and the man in the moon
"When you coming home, son?" "I don't know when
But we'll get together then, dad
You know we'll have a good time then."
I've long since retired, and my son's moved away
I called him up just the other day
I said, "I'd like to see you if you don't mind."
He said, "I'd love to, dad, if I could find the time
You see, my new job's a hassle, and the kid's got the flu
But it's sure nice talking to you, dad
It's been sure nice talking to you."
And as I hung up the phone, it occurred to me
He'd grown up just like me
My boy was just like me
And the cat's in the cradle and the silver spoon
Little boy blue and the man in the moon
"When you coming home, son?" "I don't know when
But we'll get together then, dad
We're gonna have a good time then."

Songwriters: CHAPIN, HARRY F./CHAPIN, SANDY

Bob never really knew Harry Chapin, but his song became an important part of Bob's life. Bob talks about how his father would mention the song multiple times in their long distance conversations once Bob became an adult, and a father himself. His Dad was a draftsman who kept very busy providing for his family. It seemed like no time before Bob had graduated from high school and was off to college away from home. Even though he never missed one of Bob's football games, his father would often quote the lyrics to this song and lament the fact that he hadn't spent enough time with Bob while he was growing up. Bob was sad his dad felt this way, but he never really gave it serious thought – until after his dad died. Bob might have felt much differently about things back then, had it not been for his grandparents.

Today Bob believes and promotes through public speaking and leadership seminars something he calls "eldership." He believes that many young people today lack purpose, and often don't feel like anyone cares. There are more and more children in fatherless homes. Bob knows children need elders, and elders need children. Eldership is the ability to provide wisdom and sagaciousness, the opportunity to pass on our experiences to the generation coming up behind us, or even twice removed (multi-generational) behind us. Elders listen, teach, encourage, and share with those who are their younger rising generations. They laugh and celebrate, cry and grieve, dream and realize – together.

Bob remembers growing up closer to his grandparents than most other kids his age. These are good memories,

Elders listen, teach, encourage, and share with those who are their younger rising generations. They laugh and celebrate, cry and grieve, dream and realize - together.

allowing Bob to have close elder relationships in the absence of his father at times. He wanted his own kids to have the same kind of loving relationship with their grandparents. Unfortunately, life doesn't always work the way we want it to. Because of work opportunities, Bob and his family ended up being separated from his parents by 3,000 miles, which meant his son and daughter had very little contact with their grandparents. His children didn't really seem to notice this was a missing factor in their lives, but Bob did. He knew there was a gap in their experiences and wisdom foundation that only grandparents, or the "elder" generation, can fill. He made the conscious decision that when he had his own grandkids, he would have a close relationship with them. And most of the time this requires commitment and some work.

Today Bob has those grandchildren. To promote this elder relationship with their grandparents, Bob and his wife Mary bought a piece of property jointly with his daughter and her husband. His daughter's family lives in the "big" house while Bob and Mary live in the apartment over the garage. Bob says this arrangement might not have worked as well as it does if they lived there all the time. Fortunately Bob and Mary travel frequently. But when they are home, their two granddaughters take full advantage of it. Bob has made sure the girls have full access to their grandparents. Every morning their front door opens and in run Reese and

Isabel to have breakfast together with Grandma and Papa. They know they can find their favorite cereals and snacks, especially yogurt covered raisins. When those raisins aren't there, someone is in big trouble. Isabel and Reese have perfected the *"why-aren't-there-any-yogurt-raisins?"* look. And they usually know the answer. Papa ate them.

This together time happens several times a day when everyone is home. If you called Bob at home, you would most likely hear the sounds of squealing, delighted grandchildren in the background. Everyone has their established "places" in Bob and Mary's apartment home – each has his or her own special chair or place to snuggle, and Bob is grateful his place is in a loving, close relationship with his grandkids. He always wants them to have a safe place, to come and sit with Papa, where they can tell their stories and he and Mary can tell theirs.

Bob's greatest desire now, as he watches his grandkids grow up quickly, is to have an even more established relationship with Reese and Isabel, his health allowing, once the girls reach their adulthood. He knows this relationship won't last forever, at least not in its current state, but thanks to social media he also knows he will always have "face" time with them – either on his lap, or in cyberspace. Keeping this relationship vital requires focus and attention, so that those treasured moments don't just slip away. For Bob it meant being proactive, taking intentional steps and making certain sacrifices to be sure this multi-generational bond could be developed. He does not wish to sing his father's lament, nor have his grandchildren identify with the final stanzas of Harry Chapin's song. In the meantime, Bob continues to promote multi-generational relationships, not only in his own household, but wherever people find them. He hopes, and believes, there is a movement back toward these time honored and valuable connections between our elders and the generations that follow. The richness and success of our future depends on it.

Chapter

Six

GranGran and Shannon

Shannon learned about the importance of elder relationships through a sudden, tragic loss. In the winter of her 8th grade, her dad's mother died with no warnings and no goodbyes. Her grandfather on her dad's side had already passed. Shannon remembers sitting through memorial services hearing about her grandparents from other people who knew them well. She realized then, too late, that she *didn't* know them, and had no real connection. That sudden thought, in Shannon's words, *"bummed me out."* She had to learn about her grandparents after they were gone. She realized the incredible lessons to be learned from her elder generation and how beneficial those could be for both generations. A remarkable lesson to learn for one so young. A lesson that would change her life.

After experiencing the loss of both grandparents on her father's side, without any real soul connection, Shannon was determined to not let that happen with her remaining grandparents. She stepped out to intentionally establish that link with her mother's mom, GranGran. It was truly important to Shannon to learn from her grandmother just how she was able to raise seven children, including one severely mentally and physically disabled, and still build a lasting and devoted relationship with each of her children. She did the day-to-day much on her own, as her husband's senior executive role required him to travel extensively. Shannon wanted to know how her grandmother accomplished these things, and did them so gracefully and successfully, while she was still alive. She knew these were the kind of life lessons and wisdom you couldn't really get anywhere else. At least not on such a personal level.

She knew these were the kind of life lessons and wisdom you couldn't really get anywhere else.

In her freshman year in high school, Shannon decided she wanted to go live during the summer with her grandparents in New Hampshire, and work near where they lived. She moved there and spent all summer with them. Shannon admits she had a fear of them dying soon like her other grandparents whom she never really got to know. Each time she went there, she always had a little anxiety that it might be the last time. Shannon remembers writing her grandmother a note and placing it on her pillow, thanking them for the summer together. GranGran had already written back – the note was in Shannon's suitcase when she returned home. Shannon decided she would love to continue the relationship by sharing letters, becoming pen pals of a sort. Part of Shannon wanted something to physically remind her of her grandmother, and she remembers that her handwriting was so beautiful.

It's been more than five years since that loving letter relationship began and Shannon keeps all of those notes in a special box. She cherishes each one. She and GranGran have shared their hearts, deepest thoughts and desires and their very souls in those letters. Word by word, letter by letter, Shannon knows her grandmother better and better. Shannon has a hard time describing how much those letters mean to her. Those emotions are beyond words.

One thing Shannon has noticed – her relationship with her GranGran is different than that with any of GranGran's other 19 grandchildren. Shannon believes it is the effort she puts into the relationship. She gets teased sometimes that she is GranGran's favorite. It is well known in her family that she and GranGran have something special. But they have that "something" because of Shannon's efforts. It was important enough to her to *do* something, and not just sigh and allow opportunities to pass her by – until they were gone forever. Her parents did a good job of instilling the importance of family, but it still requires a heart desire and intentional actions to make these important relationships grow. Shannon puts this same effort into maintaining and growing the relationships she has with other members of her family, including her many cousins. Whether multi-generational or same-generational, relationships requirement commitment and work. You will reap what you sow.

Shannon says that her aunts told her that GranGran benefited a great deal from Shannon's first visit during the summer, continuing through their pen pal days. GranGran's memory had started to fade a bit, and her health was not great. But when Shannon came for the summer, and the relationship continued through the post office, Shannon's aunts said there was a noticeable change. GranGran seemed to have more energy, was more talkative, upbeat, remembering things better, and had a little more spark to her. Even today, while her health is not perfect, the old spark is still there. Shannon has noticed over the years of letter exchange that GranGran's memory isn't perfect, and the relationship is changing, but they still manage to keep each other positive. GranGran and Shannon are SOULinks.

Letter writing has become a bit of an "old school" activity, but it is such a lovely way to remain connected, and as Shannon says, have a "piece" of that person in a tangible form. Email is wonderful, but it doesn't hold the same personal attachment. Shannon says she keeps an entire drawer full of notes and cards she can send to her GranGran. As a communications major in college now she sees this letter writing relationship as a natural for her. She loves it. Some have told her it is a chore and she shouldn't spend so much time doing it, especially in this busy time at college. She disagrees wholeheartedly. For Shannon this time is a joy and deepens her connections. Her Granddaddy Bill isn't left out of this special connection. Shannon also writes to him occasionally and they talk a lot on the phone. Shannon credits her grandparents for showing – *demonstrating* – how to balance intellect and emotion, business and personal lives, and also how to build family and community, all valuable lessons. And Shannon will remember these lessons.

Recently, during Spring Break, Shannon decided to go to Florida to be with her grandparents, instead of traveling to Hawaii with her friends. That was a tough decision, but the right one. During that stay, Shannon learned another, more difficult, life lesson – what Shannon calls a reality check. At a restaurant for dinner, GranGran had a seizure and passed out. Shannon had to call 911 and they took her to the hospital. In those years when all young people seem to think life goes on the same way as always, reality smacked Shannon in the race. GranGran wouldn't be around forever. Although she recovered from this incident, Shannon had a tough Spring Break that year, realizing hard truths and learning that each moment must be valued and celebrated. She may not have her grandparents with her for much longer. And now Shannon had a new mission. Tell others about this relationship. Tell them what they are missing. Inspire them to do the same with their elders and loved ones. And she does. Everywhere she goes, Shannon talks about her relationship with her GranGran. She encourages others to give their grandparents more room in their lives. She even provides easy ways to do it – *just call them while you are walking to class!* Just do it.

She is determined to be there in the end, and is well aware that loving an elder is taking a risk. Your heart will break when they are gone.

The only challenges Shannon relates about this relationship are the distance, and the "goodbyes." Those are the worst. Shannon knows one day will come for a final goodbye. Anticipating that day, Shannon has even formulated a plan if she is away from home when it happens. So much of her identity today, and tomorrow, is in GranGran. She is determined to be there in the end, and is well aware that loving an elder is taking a risk. Your heart will break when they are gone. But to her it is worth every single moment, every minute given, every tear shed, and every laugh shared.

Shannon even credits her relationship with GranGran for getting her into college. Perhaps that is an overstatement, but not to Shannon. She had to write an essay about herself as part of the admissions process for college. She has graciously allowed me to share this with you. I hope you hear the heart of a young lady who has learned the tremendous value of not only family, but the wisdom of elders.

> *As I sit down to write this essay I can see out of the corner of my eye a box peeking out from underneath my bed. This box is more than just an old shoebox, it holds some of the most meaningful words that have ever been shared with me. This box represents the importance of family.*
>
> *I was very lucky to learn the importance of relationships early in middle school. Tragically, this knowledge came through the sudden death of my grandfather. My Dad's father, Grandpa, died in December of 2008; there was no warning and there were no goodbyes. After losing my grandpa, I realized how quickly God can take someone away from you. This was the first time I truly became aware of how important family bonds are.*

With this new awareness, I decided that I wanted to get to know my grandma better, so when my family visited her in Florida that spring, I spent every moment I could with her. Sadly, two months later, in June, my grandma became very sick. Two nights before she died, I wrote my first and last letter to Grandma. I shared my sincere gratitude to her for creating our whole family and I apologized that I had not learned the importance of family bonds soon enough. The day before she died, Grandma wrote me a letter in which she told me she was proud of me, and the young lady I was becoming and that I am a credit to our family. To this day, this letter is framed and hanging in my room, just below a photo of the two of us, when I was a toddler and she was tickling me on our deck.

Grandma's letter changed my life in many ways. One of the most important things it did was to begin a wonderful and fulfilling relationship with my Mom's mother, GranGran. Later that summer, after Grandma passed away, I asked GranGran if she wanted to become pen pals. GranGran and I have been sending greeting cards, uplifting words, and long letters to each other once or twice a week for the past three and a half years. I have saved all of the 170 letters in a box under my bed and take them out to read whenever I am feeling down or just miss her. The importance of these letters in my life is something that words cannot even describe. I am so grateful for the deep, caring, loving relationship I now have with GranGran, thanks to these letters. We are by each other's side whenever possible, we know and understand each other, and we truly love one another. This is the most precious gift I have received from my experiences with my two grandmothers: to understand how to love deeply. The simple action of sitting down and writing a letter has become one of the most meaningful moments of my busy weeks. It is my dream that someday after I am long gone my grandchildren will thumb through my box of letters and learn about the wonderful relationship I had with their great-great-grandmother. I hope they do this and learn from them the same lesson they taught me: Family is truly what life is all about.

Shannon continues today to be an ambassador-at-large for multi-generational relationships. Her life has been, and will continue to be, shaped by the wisdom of her family and her elders. That's exactly how it should be.

Chapter

Charles, Barbara and Coffee Beans

Charles and Barbara have seven grandchildren, whom they say keep them young, important, relevant and needed. They have chosen to be as actively involved in each of their lives as possible. They believe you can't ever spend too much time with the younger generations. Charles and Barbara also believe in showing their grandchildren how special they are in unique gifts. When each of their grandchildren turned 12, they took them anywhere in America the grandchild wanted to go, for one week. Spending this committed time together has allowed wonderful things to happen, and for relationships to be cemented for life.

This family also believes that one of the greatest gifts that can be given to any young person is to show them other parts of the world. Life is different, people are different, cultural values are different. These experiences help young people develop the skills for a life of wise decision making. When their four oldest grandchildren were in their teens, Barbara and Charles were able to go on a mission trip to

Kenya together. These young people now have a much broader, and more sober, view of the world than most in their generation.

When you make the effort to know others better, make them understand they are important to you, they will return the sentiment and come to cherish you as well. This is true in every relationship, and most especially in multi-generational bonds. Charles and Barbara know that certain skills and mindsets can grow these relationships into lifetime opportunities for a mutual exchange of joys, values and growth – in both generations. One of the most important of these multi-generational guidelines, for both generations, is to love the other right where they are. And, just as importantly, perhaps the greatest skill is to listen – truly hear what the other is saying, not just with your ears, but with your heart. Unlike some other relationships, multi-generational relationships can easily reach a place of relaxation because you don't have to maintain being something you are not. You are not a parent responsible for this person's upbringing and training. You are not a boss, judge or police officer keeping the peace. You are a *safe* place. You are a SOULink.

All these years of building wonderful and productive relationships with their seven grandchildren actually prepared Charles and Barbara for one of the grandest adventures of their lives. The skills, attitudes, and relational approaches used to fashion lifetime links with grandchildren also work well with coffee plantation workers in a different country. Through an interesting series of events, Charles and Barbara found themselves living on a coffee plantation in Cyimbili, Rwanda. They didn't know the people, didn't know the culture, and knew absolutely nothing about coffee beans. Charles knew business. He is a retired successful businessman, and he and his wife Barbara were seeking a place to use their experiences, skills, knowledge and gifts. Charles and Barbara were beyond seeking success - they were pursuing significance instead. Through prayer and divine direction, they were asked to use those gifts to revitalize a coffee plantation in Africa. No one saw that coming!

Cyimbili is located on the shores of Lake Kivu in Western Rwanda. Its beautiful lush hills were once the home of one of Africa's largest and well-established coffee plantations, producing about 100,000 pounds of coffee each year. The plantation provided sustainable jobs and economic stability for this community and region. In addition to coffee, the plantation also served the local people through its schools, church and many social services.

But all this came to a screeching halt in 1994. The Rwandan genocidal wars forever scarred the country of Rwanda, and devastated the coffee plantation. In just 100 days, 800,000 people were killed, leaving many others homeless and without even the basic needs of food, water and shelter. The village of Cyimbili was abandoned in ruin, and the coffee plantation was deserted, left to sit and decay.

Célestin, a young man who grew up and graduated from the plantation high school in Cyimbili, never forgot his childhood or the once thriving coffee plantation. He later established an African ministry that works to develop servant leaders through reconciliation, to transform the war-ravaged communities in East and Central Africa. Célestin personally experienced the horrors of genocide when members of his own family, his home church and village, were murdered in revenge killings.

Through many years, many prayers, many tears and many partnerships, Célestin and his group have worked to restore and rehabilitate the once prosperous coffee plantation. Infrastructure has been built, skilled people brought in to terrace and shape the land properly, establish schools and medical clinics, and plant more than 40,000 coffee trees – among other things. This has been a 5-year commitment by many people and organizations. The plantation has been restored, is fully operational and is quite an active place these days. But the pieces hadn't all come together yet. Business practices in Africa sometimes leave a bit to be desired.

Barbara was a bit surprised the first time she heard the greeting *"You are so old and so fat!"*

And here is the open door to not only multi-generational relationships, but multi-cultural adventures for Charles and Barbara. Célestin, Charles and Barbara had met through the ministry's American offices. Knowing Charles was a successful businessman, Célestin tapped him and his wife on the shoulder to bring those business practices to Cyimbili. He knew a good match when he saw one. It took some time, but finally Charles and Barbara were there, among a people they didn't know, a language they didn't speak, and a culture completely foreign. And, to add to this mix, all the workers on the plantation were of a much younger generation. Charles and Barbara are in their 70s, retired white folk thrust in a sea of much younger black faces who had very little good experience with the *wazungu* who had previously come to only take and never give. Célestin prepared these Africans to receive the white older folk as graciously as they could. Barbara says Célestin was wasting his breath, because from the moment they arrived, they were so lovingly and tenderly cared for they felt like family.

Even so, Barbara was a bit surprised the first time she heard the greeting *"You are so old and so fat!"* Well, that's obviously not something we would want to hear in our culture. But to Africans, it is an extreme compliment. Age is likened to wisdom, and fat to resources and wealth. For the most part, the older generation is revered by Rwandans. It took awhile, but Barbara came to love it when they called her old and fat. And she even learned to say "thank you" in response. Eventually, the short form of this compliment morphed into the Rwandans calling Barbara *"old mama,"* a term of endearment for a grandmother.

Charles and Barbara instituted some business changes quickly, which helped provide the final missing piece in making this plantation successful. For example, when they set up their first business meeting the next day after arriving, at 3:00 pm, only one person was there at 3:00 pm. One by one they filtered in, some as late as an hour. There was absolutely no concept of time lines and time management. But this journey was not so much about business practices, at least not for Charles and Barbara, as it was about establishing some of the richest multi-generational and multi-cultural relationships one could ever imagine.

The ministries administrating the operation of the plantation had hired a young man to be the plantation manager. Nepo was a former teacher and had zero knowledge about coffee, or what it takes to make a successful plantation. But Nepo had leadership qualities and a desire to learn. Charles and Barbara saw this immediately and began mentoring Nepo. He would come have dinner with them and they would sit for hours on the porch, talking and laughing together. Little by little cultural and generational boundaries began to fall away. And little by little, Nepo practiced and polished his leadership skills. Nepo became the "go to" person on the plantation, even graciously and efficiently handling such things as the tragic deaths of two young boys who drowned in the nearby lake. Nepo has become the leader of not only a coffee plantation, but also his entire community. He has taught himself everything there is to know about growing coffee and making a plantation successful. Most of Rwanda grows a grade B or even C coffee, but Cyimbili is striving for the best, a premium coffee not offered anywhere else in Africa.

Getting the right people in place has been a great part of the strategy, including a knowledgeable trained local agronomist and a maintenance person who actually knows how to fix things. But putting the people in place was only the beginning. Charles and Barbara nurtured and mentored these people to make them the best coffee growers they can be – and make them the best *people* they can be. Throughout the process they have employed all those things that have worked so well with their grandchildren – acceptance, a listening ear and heart, and the wisdom only age affords.

No matter the circumstances or the place, some practices and attitudes work wherever relationships live, even in places where language is not a common denominator. Barbara fondly remembers Anastasia, the lady who cooked for the working camp. Anastasia didn't speak a lick of English, and Barbara had no understanding of Anastasia's language. One day Nepo came into Barbara and Charles' living quarters to find Barbara entertaining Anastasia with tea. Nepo stopped dead in his tracks and laughingly proclaimed, *"How can you all visit? You can't even talk!"* That never stopped them.

When Charles and Barbara first arrived, their living quarters, if you could call it that, consisted of a run-down neglected former missionary's house with holes in the bright orange walls, a leaky roof, sporadic electrical power, and the only water supply brown contaminated muddy river water. Barbara and Anastasia made curtains together to provide privacy and cleaned and restored this "house" to a somewhat habitable state. Barbara and Anastasia would also work puzzles together, where words aren't needed. By the time Charles and Barbara left Cyimbili, both Anastasia and Barbara cried together. Tears, laughter and acceptance don't depend upon words.

Charles and Barbara also realized quickly that Anastasia did not cook for them, only the workers. They were on their own, and if you were hungry, you had to eat what you grew. That meant a garden and learning what grew and how to grow it in this strange place. Once again, Anastasia came to the rescue. In the beginning Charles and Barbara's diet changed drastically, eating only what they grew out of the garden. There was no meat available in Cyimbili. For that you had to travel five hours to Kigali over a treacherous road across a steep mountain range. Needless to say, that trip didn't happen too often. After only a month in Cyimbili, both Charles and Barbara lost 25 pounds. Eventually, with help of the plantation workers, they learned how to eat what they could grow and supplement that every so often with a few tidbits of beef or chicken as it was available.

As the days flew by the coffee plantation became more productive, more streamlined, and more profitable to the people who worked there, and the community as a whole. Charles is the first to admit that while he may have instituted some very sound American business practices to assist this plantation into the twenty-first century of business and profit, he also learned much from the African way of doing things. One of those lessons is very foreign to Americans. In our culture, when you greet someone you do so quickly and nicely and then move on, also quickly. But in Africa, when you greet someone and ask how they are, you need to be prepared to actually spend time with them and learn how they *really* are, and *who* they really are. Africans sit down upon greeting, not move onto the next meeting with a quick handshake and painted smile. They want to know you. They want to hear about you.

Most Africans have had bad experiences with those "white people" called *mzungu* (or *wazungu*, plural). They come smiling, but leave taking everything. It took some time to build trust in this place, but with many sit-down "greetings" and long talks after dinner on the front porch viewing the beautiful African skies at night, trust was established. There are some things much more important than time.

The Rwandans respected and trusted these *wazungu,* originally because age means wisdom. But mostly, as they came to know and accept one another right where they were, Barbara and Charles were trusted because they proved they *could* be trusted. Even though there was somewhat of a language barrier, listening with ears and heart paved the way for understanding. Again, the same skills and mindset that work with grandchildren also work wonders with African coffee farmers. They learned to laugh at their differences and rejoice in their similarities.

Barbara knew that the diet in Cyimbili would be drastically different than what they were used to, so she came prepared with packed goodies to allow them little treats here and there. That included brownie mixes and popcorn, which she decided to share one night with the workers. It would be their special treat, a gift to them. When visiting many foreign cultures, they tell you never refuse to eat anything offered, that this would be considered rude. When something was offered, you ate it, no matter what. So the opposite must be true as well. If a foreigner offers you something different, you eat it. Well, not always. Charles and Barbara think of brownies and popcorn as treats, something special. One worker, however, refused to eat them. He didn't speak English, so they asked someone why this man would not eat their special food gifts. They asked if he knew what it was they offered. The other man said yes,

Relationships suffer in the absence of complete honesty.

he knew, but those things were children's food. An adult did not eat food for children! They all just laughed, and permission was granted to everyone to be totally honest with one another. This could have been another potential cultural stumbling block. Total honesty can be perceived in many ways, especially if it is not lovingly and carefully given. But relationships suffer in the absence of complete honesty, whether multi-generational or multi-cultural. So many things could have gotten in the way of this rich and successful mentorship of neophyte coffee farmers from a different culture, speaking a different language. But acceptance, listening, honesty and loads of laughter have gotten this plantation back on track.

As a result of one of those head-scratching amazing and divinely orchestrated turn of events, a week after Charles and Barbara accepted the call to go to Cyimbili, they got another call, from their oldest grandson Cameron, who was finishing up college at Stanford. *"Grandma, the strangest thing just happened. I got a job offer today."* Great, where is it? *"Rwanda!"* As it turned out, Cameron was working in Rwanda just two hours away from Charles and Barbara while they were in Cyimbili. They were able to visit frequently, even taking Cameron to dinner in "town" for his birthday. When they returned, Cameron was treated to a beautiful display of African warmth and acceptance – they gave him a surprise birthday party complete with candy, homemade gifts and the youth of the village.

So, was it a coincidence that the skills Barbara and Charles first honed in their relationships with their grandchildren were critically useful in their multi-generational and multi-cultural relationships with the Cyimbili people? Was it a coincidence that their oldest grandson Cameron actually was there working in Rwanda at the same time they were? Well, you know what the Jewish rabbis say, *"Coincidence is not a kosher word!"*

Today the Cyimbili Coffee Plantation is fully operational, providing employment for almost two hundred local people among 40,000 coffee trees, all working hard to produce Africa's premium coffee. At the website for this plantation, there is a caption that reads. *"Coffee Changes Lives."* For those who have benefited from this revived coffee plantation, that is literally true. However, we would like to clarify this a bit. It isn't coffee that changes lives, it's *people who change lives.* No matter what generation, no matter what city or country, no matter what language. People change lives. People change people. Barbara and Charles changed the lives of those running an African coffee plantation, but the plantation workers changed Charles and Barbara as well. They learned that God's people are God's people, everywhere, every age, every generation, every language, every shared goal. People are people.

And when you are in Cyimbili, if you like and respect someone you hold their hand. It is a symbol of linked souls. Charles and Barbara will never forget those moments of walking and talking, hand in hand, with their SOULinks from a different era, on another continent.

Changing the world is good for those
who want their names in books.
But being happy, that is for those who
write their names in the lives of others,
and hold the hearts of others
as the treasures most dear.

Orson Scott Card

Chapter

Dorothy and Her Court

Dorothy was holding court. She sat on a large colorful couch surrounded by a half dozen little faces completely absorbed in Dorothy's story. She didn't read from a book. She was relating her personal stories about her flying adventures. The sometimes halting words were punctuated by grand hand and arm gestures, animated expressions and a wonderfully gleeful smile. Her story kept her very young listeners on the edge of their seats. Well, on the edge of the floor, where they sat in front of her. Heads resting on little hands, eyes following Dorothy's movements with rapt attention, her listeners were enthralled. They didn't understand all the words, but that didn't matter one bit to them.

Dorothy had lots of stories. She served with the U. S. Army Nurse Corps in South Korea during the Korean War. She was a flight nurse, flying hundreds of missions to evacuate the wounded often in very dangerous situations. Dorothy was one of an elite group of nurses specially trained and commissioned to fly in MEDEVAC aircraft.

Dorothy dodged danger and endured hardship in order to save the lives of hundreds of wounded soldiers. During these flights Dorothy would make sure these soldiers were safe and their medical needs given her full attention. It took a special brand of courage to serve her country in this way. Many nurses died in this service, often in aircraft crashes. Yes, Dorothy indeed had her stories. Dorothy is 84 years old. Her audience this day was about 80 years behind her.

This wouldn't seem on the surface to be anything unusual, a woman war veteran telling amazing stories of heroism and danger during her flight nurse career. But what we don't immediately see here is that Dorothy has advanced Alzheimer's disease. And prior to her introduction to this very young willing group of listeners Dorothy could barely string words together to form a coherent sentence.

After the war, Dorothy married her husband Douglas, also a Korean War veteran, and went on to have four wonderful children *(all with names beginning with the letter "D," of course)* and a beautiful life full of grandchildren and great-grandchildren. Until about eight years ago, when Douglas began seeing signs that something was wrong. His wonderful courageous wife of sixty years was often confused, and her memory was failing. After ignoring many of these symptoms for a long while Douglas finally knew they had to see a doctor, and his worst fears were confirmed. Dorothy indeed had Alzheimer's and it was getting worse. Douglas wanted to keep his wife at home as long as possible, but soon she couldn't communicate even the most basic of thoughts or needs, and she failed to recognize close friends and even her grandchildren.

Douglas could no longer care for his wife alone. With a very heavy heart, he made arrangements for Dorothy to live in a special retirement home that specialized in Alzheimer's care. Douglas had done his homework and researched all the available facilities. He believed he had made the right choice for Dorothy.

One of the contributing factors in Douglas' decision was the fact that this particular care facility had a very unique environment. When the managers of this retirement center formulated their plans, they wanted to make the setting for their patients as home-like as possible. Nothing in this place brings to mind an institution or clinic. It has the look and feel of home. But they believed that one thing was missing to really make this place feel like a warm and typical home – children. It is not the prevailing thinking to combine the very old, especially those suffering from Alzheimer's or dementia, with the very young. But that is precisely what this group did. They designed and built a fully functioning preschool on the premises. This area is light and inviting, bright and bold and busy. It features large windows all around which enable the residents to view, and during specially designed interactive opportunities, to engage with these three- and four-year-olds. The results have been jaw-dropping, literally.

The planners of this facility envisioned some wonderful intergenerational sharing times, beneficial to both the older residents and the young energetic preschoolers. And that's what happened, but no one was prepared for what else they observed.

In specially designed "share and play times," residents come into this lively environment where sometimes as many as forty kids buzz around in typical preschool energy and controlled chaos. Initially the plan was for the older generation to merely be present, to enjoy the wonderful vitality of preschoolers. They knew intergenerational relationships are very uplifting with wonderful mutual benefits. But they had no idea that these would also be spontaneously *interactive.* No one expected this, but gradually the patients began to speak to the kids, even taking part in whatever activity the little ones were doing – coloring, making sandwiches for the whole group, telling stories, playing games.

A non-communicative, confused elder would enter the room, but would shortly become lucid, talking and engaging with three-year-olds.

Patients like Dorothy, who previously could not connect her words to form whole sentences, began speaking for the first time. They started asking questions, making comments and more importantly, making *sense*. Both the preschool workers and the facility practitioners were shocked. What they were seeing was miraculous. And this wasn't just a one-time phenomenon. This happened over and over again. A non-communicative, confused elder would enter the room, but would shortly become lucid, talking and engaging with three-year olds.

Doctors and researchers don't yet know exactly what happens in this process, or why. They speculate that something in these little ones triggers a long-buried response. It resurrects old memories of mothers and fathers and child rearing years. And in Dorothy's case, those wonderful adventures flying wounded soldiers out of South Korea.

Intergenerational relationships are rich with mutual beneficial potential for everyone. The parents of these little preschoolers say their kids love their elder friends and play with them as they would play with someone their own age. They see nothing out of the ordinary – just another treasured playmate, with whom they are extraordinarily patient. Children of Alzheimer's and dementia patients are beyond joyful when they see these interactive breakthroughs. These kinds of facilities are not the mainstream retirement residences, or even typical Alzheimer's facilities, but the amazing results of bringing the very old together with the very young have been so dramatic and so well-received that these kinds of communities are found more and more, in places like West Seattle, Washington, Hatfield, Pennsylvania, Eagan, Minnesota, and Portland, Oregon, to name just a few.

Before the last century families generally stayed together, if not in the same house at least in the same community. The very young were often cared for by the very old. Aging elders were cared for by their younger generations and families aged in place as a symbiotic intergenerational unit. Perhaps this is why Alzheimer's and dementia were not as prevalent in those days. We function better, in every way, when generations interact and are interdependent. Multi-generational relationships make every area of life – *body, mind and spirit* – better, richer, more complete.

A few feet away from Dorothy and her rapt audience, Carl sat at a table helping Amadeo build a grand fortress. Amadeo was the architect of this Lego masterpiece, giving Carl careful instructions, telling him of his dreams and designs for this plastic citadel. Carl followed Amadeo's patient instruction. Carl didn't always do it right, and Amadeo would stop and turn full face to Carl and explain it again in slow, distinctly enunciated words. Carl would try again, and when he got it right, Amadeo would clap. Carl's grin brought tears to his 52-year old son's eyes as he watched from the other side of the window. The master architect on this project was 4 years old. Carl is in his seventies.

As Douglas watches his wife's animated face while she tells her listeners of her early days of flying, he is certain he made the right choice in care facilities for his beloved flight nurse bride.

Chapter

Jim and Dreadlocks

Inside the carpeted and cubicled halls of SS&T Corporation a serious problem threatened the future of this successful, old and established bastion of business. Everyone in business knows that employee retention is one of the biggest issues affecting the all-important bottom line. But for some reason, so far unknown to the executives and strategy makers at SS&T, this was becoming a difficult and losing battle. Lack of talent wasn't the issue. Goodness knows there were very bright and energetic workers out there, flooding the HR departments of corporate America in droves. The issue was not *finding* these new employees. The issue was *keeping* them. This problem was not just the bane of this particular corporation. Businesses everywhere were experiencing this phenomenon. *But why?*

The CEO and Board of SS&T put their heads together, acknowledging the problem, seeking to find the answers, and craft a solution. One man, a top level executive, was appointed to find out why the younger generation of workers didn't last long in their corporate positions, and more importantly, what changes could be made to insure their longevity and the future success of SS&T. He was tasked with a major redesign of SS&T's working environment and standard business practices. And thus began James' journey, an adventure that would take him to places, and people, he never expected.

One of the first things Jim *(James was just too formal, too businesslike, for this project)* discovered was that these younger workers had a moniker – they were called "Millennials." Some even had the odd title of Gen-X or Gen Y. He also learned that one generation had been called "The Greatest Generation." Well, that was James' parents' generation, and if they were the "greatest" generation, what did that make him? Of all the ridiculous things, he was a member of the "Baby Boomers" generation. Wow, those folks out there who make their living crafting creative titles for anything and everything *(we do love our labels!)* sure had interesting imaginations. Alright, we have labels for our generations. Now what? Jim committed himself to finding out what made those generations different, and how they can work together for longer than just a few months. He continued to research the generations and their proverbial "gaps" trying to identify differences and commonalities.

Jim then determined he would immerse himself in the younger generation. He started hanging out in coffee shops and seeking conversation with these young people. He attended events that attracted them. He committed to being among them wherever they could be found. They had strange sounding labels, and initially Jim considered *them* strange, too. Their values were different. Their dress was different. Their talk was different, and their priorities were different. To Jim, they might as well have been aliens from another planet. He wasn't sure he was going to be able to create any bridges in this people-gap project.

But Jim kept at it. Along the way in his quest for answers, Jim met some real "characters," as he called them, but also learned that these foreigners and aliens were just people, like him, with similar values, just expressed differently. He met Matthew, whose daily uniform was sandals, socks, holey jeans and a T-shirt that screamed something that Jim couldn't quite understand. But Matthew's knowledge of what worked and what didn't in business was incredible. He had the most awesome sense of human dynamics. And Ashley, one of the most creative and sharp minds he had ever encountered, an amazingly bright wit and innovator who was also an amazingly committed mother to her new baby and family. Jim met Emily at an outdoor concert one day. He found out Emily was a dare devil, one of those younger "kids" who were fearless — an adventure junkie. She jumped out of airplanes and was a treasure hunter and deep sea diver. Amazingly, he also found out that Emily was a sharp and successful young attorney. Jim remembers a long conversation he and Emily had about life balance, another strange concept in corporate America. And then there was the guy with a 27-letter name no one could pronounce and everyone called "Ted" *(one of the many syllables in his name)* whose financial acumen was bar none. Oh, can't forget Mung, yes that was really his name, the guy who enlightened Jim about dreadlocks *(intentionally matted and sculpted "ropes" of hair...really??),* and over-the-top knowledge and understanding of the global marketplace.

Wow, SS&T needed these guys. But what did *they* need? With time, these bright minds were more than an alien generation, these were Jim's friends. They initially looked at him as being just as weird as he saw them at first. Soon, however, all saw each other as bright, talented people. Friends and fellow human beings, all needing the same things – acknowledgment, respect and an environment that stimulated those bright minds. They all realized that you just need to care enough about the "aliens among us" to get to know them. The differences are still there, but they can be celebrated, and are no longer barriers.

What Jim learned at the end of his "project" is that SS&T was a typical big American corporation with the same look and feel as most in this country. Offices were in neat little boxes in neat little rows with neat little amenities, but not too much. For the most part they are stark and sterile. The dress code is just as neat, stark and sterile – three-piece suits, white shirts and expensive splashy ties, a unisex uniform. There was an expected image, expected code of language and dress, and an expected commitment above and beyond everything else to the hallowed corporation. Profit was a sacred word and a sacred pursuit. And everyone was expected to make their life passion and priority that pursuit. This is the way business started, and the way business has been conducted for centuries.

Now enter the Millennials, and the Gen-Y's and the Gen-X's. Something happened in the gene pool, who knows *what*, but these guys and gals did not seem to understand, much less enjoy, the corporate way. They didn't enjoy neat little boxes, and suits and ties were those things that cut off your airway and made you chafe and squirm during family photos. They didn't enjoy giving up all their time to the corporation. They didn't want to give up their family or fun time to seal the deal no matter when, no matter how, no matter what. In fact, they seemed to enjoy life over business. Now that truly was a foreign concept to Jim's generation and Jim's corporation. For generations business has been conducted in the same stuffy way, by stuffed shirts and stuffed agendas and calendars. But it became very obvious to Jim that things would have to change in order to attract and retain the incredible new talent and intellect available to corporations like SS&T.

They didn't enjoy neat little boxes, and suits and ties were those things that cut off your airway and made you chafe and squirm during family photos.

After many hours, days and months of Jim's research, which eventually became more of a life adventure and joyful journey than a business project, Jim took his findings and recommendations back to the boardroom at SS&T. They were shocked when they saw Jim. You see, during this journey Jim had inadvertently redesigned *himself*. He started wearing colored shirts, no ties, and casual slacks *(he did decide it was probably not appropriate to wear his holey jeans into the hallowed board chambers).* His hair was styled "young" and fresh. He was no longer the image expected in the corporate inner sanctum. *What had happened to James?*

Little by little Jim came to realize that Millennials liked living life, and he kind of liked that, too. They had a passion for life instead of a passion for profit. And they could do amazing things, but not in the environment offered by corporate America. They came, they saw...and then they left. How to conquer this? The one word everyone seems to hate...*change*. Jim knew that in order to provide the environment that would maximize the amazing potential among these younger generations, to retain them and their talent, the cubicles and the suits would have to be discarded along the highway to the future. And so would the expectations of business before all other life needs.

We don't like change. It makes us cringe. *"But we've always done it this way!"* is screamed as we are dragged into change. Jim did his own screaming. He argued with himself and he argued with his executive team. A lot of sputtering about changing the corporate environment came from the board room at SS&T. But eventually these sons and daughters of the "greatest generation" realized they had no choice. They had to acknowledge and even embrace the change, and actively seek to create an environment, and the appropriate set of perks, that appealed to these talented younger workers. Their successful future depended on it. And so they did. They jumped into this change with both feet, nothing held back – tradition be, well, you know. Enter the days of ping pong tables and rock climbing walls, daycare, real days off, and lattes, for starters. Gone the days of neat little boxes all in a row.

SS&T new hires found a completely changed business environment, one tailored to inspire and retain the bright minds of the Millennials, Gen-Y's, and Gen-Exers. And something else, something very interesting, happened, too. Those stuffed shirts and die-cut older corporate types began to enjoy this new environment, too. No one saw *that* coming. Production was up across the board. The mood was up, too, and so was employee retention. And another something else came with this new look and feel in the previously sacred business workplace – *relationships*. Cubicles don't encourage relationships. But openness and a more congenial environment does. The "olders" and the "youngers" starting talking more, started getting to know one another as real people, not as generations with different labels.

Jim remembers that sadly it took a tragedy for him to come to an amazing "ah ha" moment after these changes were instituted. One of the "older" executives suddenly died. Most of the employees attended his memorial service. As they stood around talking after the service, in groups not defined by age, but by love and respect for this man *(who apparently could play a mean game of ping pong)*, Jim realized that his office was no longer a workplace, it was a life-place where family lived and worked together. They had successfully built that bridge that brought the previously "estranged" generations together for mutual benefit – not just for profit, but for purpose. This was now a multi-talented, and multi-generational family that learned how to blend their values, skills and dreams together for a shared and better future.

By the way, SS&T is a real corporation, but the name I used here is not. I figured SS&T had a good corporate ring for "Stuffed Shirts and Ties." Don't you agree?

I had embraced you...
long before I hugged you.

Sanober Khan

Chapter

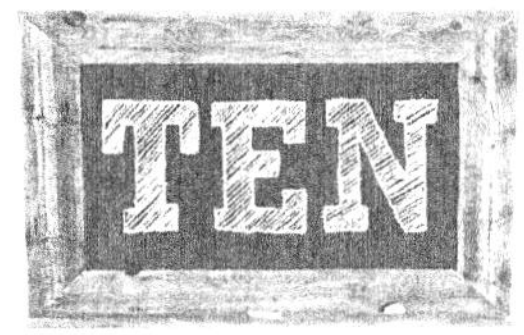

Jack's Birthday and...

John's Island is a magical place. Besides being one of *"America's Top 25 Golf Communities,"* picturesque landscapes, miles of beautiful beaches, resort-like ambience and almost perfect weather in the winter months, John's Island is a place that attracts multi-generational relationships like a magnet. Since its development began over 40 years ago, this community just north of Vero Beach, Florida has been producing amazing and enduring relationships within its now legendary family-oriented lifestyle.

Like much of Florida, John's Island is a destination of choice for those who live in the colder climates and desire a warmer place to enjoy the winter months. Many of the residents here are permanent year-round, but many others are winter residents only, living most of the year in other places scattered around the country. Every winter is like a grand reunion time as families return to their warm weather winter havens.

Shortly after John's Island was initially developed, three young girls became fast friends, playing on the beautiful beaches of this wonderful ocean playground. Their parents had all purchased winter homes in this community, and knew each other well. After many seasons of reunions and joyful romps on the beach, these girls grew up and began their own families. Sally, Joan and Patti chose to return to John's Island with *their* families because by now it was indeed "home away from home." Their little ones loved the beaches, and the people, as much as they did. And of course, this was where grandmas and grandpas lived in the winter.

December 28, 1990 was Jack's first birthday. Jack is Sally's son. No one really remembers exactly how what is now referenced as "Jack's Birthday" celebration began. Someone thought it would be a great idea to get the newest generation of winter residents together for a birthday party. This party included a table for nine at the Beach Club, for three grandmothers *(Sally, Madeleine and Cis)*, three daughters *(Joan, Sally and Patti)*, and three high chairs for Jack the birthday boy, Joan's daughter Allison 18 months old, and Patti's son Eddy 9 months old. Little did anyone know or even dream that this birthday party would become a 25 year annual tradition. What started as three multi-generational families grew into multiple families, multiple generations and multiple celebrations of birthdays and special times together.

It was very convenient, and providential, for Jack to have his birthday near Christmas. Most of these families had already established the tradition of traveling to John's

Island to spend the holidays. Instead of snow and sleigh bells they enjoyed miles of warm sandy beaches and great outdoor activities – something you just can't find in December in Massachusetts or Oregon. One year turned into the next year, and the next, and the next... It didn't start out this way, but Jack's birthday became the highlight of the year for these families, many of whom would spend the entire holiday season at John's Island, looking forward to Jack's Birthday celebration. It was the event that drew an entire new family together.

Over the years this "family" expanded – a lot. There were always games and fun on the beach. Lively father son football games attracted others looking to join the fun. Everyone, anyone passing by, was welcome to join in the rowdy play. Some of these sandy quarterbacks played one game and went their way. Others returned year after year to resume the never-ending football game on the beach. One kid walking the beach by himself was invited to join the game, and now he and his family, from Oklahoma, celebrate "Jack's Birthday" also. One winter David, about five or six years old at the time, had a skim board down at the shore. He was alone, but not for long. Others wanted to try his new toy and before you knew it, David and his family were a regular part of Jack's Birthday that year, and every year after. One of the rules of this unique multi-generational family is inclusion. This is not a private, exclusive group. NO one is excluded. Everyone is potential family. Everyone is invited. Everyone is included.

As the original moms present at Jack's first birthday party reflect on this phenomenon, they ponder whether or not these kids, now dozens of them, would have been friends if they lived in their own neighborhoods. It really doesn't matter. Somehow, in this magical place, everyone is a friend, everyone is family.

What started as three families has grown to a regular seven or eight, times three or even four generations, hailing from places like Oregon, Oklahoma, North Carolina, Georgia, Kansas and Massachusetts. A single birthday party has evolved from a table for nine *(well, six really, and three high chairs)* to dozens and dozens of people celebrating not just a birthday, but the joy of one another. While these families are obviously related within their own standard family structures, for the most part, the relationships that have grown here are not blood bonds, they are SOULinks.

One by one, year by year, other special events were added and adopted as traditional celebratory events during these days of reunion. Taco night and bowling dates have been added to the "birthday" line-up. Sleepovers and beach games are like food for hungry souls. There is always the traditional "walk on the beach." It's never planned, it just happens. One person gets up and starts to walk. Then another and another, and another. Some pair up in twos and threes. Sometimes the entire group walks the beach together, engaging in intimate friendly conversations that span the months apart, reuniting common bonds and relationships.

Taco night is one of those special times of generational crossover bonding. A typical taco night will find a college student who has found wise counsel in a beach friend's grandfather as she eats her taco and relates her latest challenges. She eagerly listens to his experienced advice. Yes, *eagerly*. She actually wants to hear what he has to say. A great-grandmother plays with another family's children, showing them games she used to play as a child. Mothers and dads laugh with kids who could be their grandkids, but aren't. *Or are they?* In this group, the blood lines have been blurred. These are SOULinks joining forces to create a new family. And in this near perfect scene, a classic advertisement for multi-generational relationships, resides another of the "rules" of this group – hospitality. Young and old participate in the often forgotten art of hosting. Taco night depends on the desire to show hospitality and do your share to make it possible. And, as usual, the older generation shares traditions, etiquette *(a dying art revived among these generations)*, tips and learned lessons.

The younger generations bring vitality, energy, eagerness to belong, and many questions needing answers that can only be provided by the wisdom of age and experience. On taco night there are no "kids" tables. Everyone is everywhere. It's the same on the beach, and for any of the other activities and events during this week. Regardless of age, every person is a valued member of this treasured family of multiple multi-generational relationships.

The important traditions of birthday cake and ice cream in the Beach Club on December 28, bowling and taco night provide the structure for this week of SOULinks strengthening. And, if some situation comes up where things can't happen as planned, a new plan is launched.

One year two families were leaving on the 28th for a cruise. The group did not want the streak of birthday celebration on the 28th to end, so instead of the usual lunch of cake and ice cream, they got together and made 40 breakfast burritos and had everyone meet at the Beach Club to celebrate early in the day, before the other families had to leave. There is always a way. As the saying goes, *"where there is a will...."*

It has been interesting, and sometimes amusing, watching the various relationships change over the years. For example, many of the children grew to have those typical teenage "crushes" on one another. And, since there was always an open invitation to join up with the group, these young people learned the hard way never to invite a boyfriend or girlfriend to meet a beach crush!

Now 25 years later, children have grown up, and others have been adopted into this family. They have attended schools at far flung places across the country, yet continue to keep in touch and fiercely support and encourage one another through the marvel of social media. They have visited one another at various other times during the year, as opportunities arise. They maintain constant and regular communication, even outside that one week in December. Some have even started their own families. Mothers have become grandmothers, and grandmothers have become great-

Multi-generational relationships may happen in surprising unplanned ways, but they are not sustained and will not continue unless the people in them want them to.

grandmothers. This extended family even added another annual event at the 4th of July holiday.

No one would even consider not coming together during the holidays for Jack's Birthday. One year Jack himself was having trouble getting his work schedule coordinated enough to make this annual family event – his own birthday! Because this is such a special time, however, he flew down to John's Island and spent only 48 hours here, but those were the most wonderful 48 hours full of richness and camaraderie. He wouldn't miss it, and neither would anyone else.

And, herein resides perhaps the most important guideline for this unique group, the one necessary ingredient that makes these relationships possible – desire and commitment. These people WANT to be together. They desire to share one another's company. They are committed to sustaining these relationships and growing them. Multi-generational relationships may happen in surprising unplanned ways, but they are not sustained and will not continue unless the people in them want them to. This is true for any relationship. And all relationships take commitment, and yes, sometimes even a little work. Jack had to do some fancy footwork to get down to John's Island for his birthday that year, but there was no way he *wasn't* going to be there, even if only for two days.

During the rest of the year the relationships continue. Long distance most of the time, but communication is always maintained. Everyone is welcome in everyone else's homes. They invest time and money in staying in touch over the course of the year. Communication may look different and take different form for each person, but it is top priority to everyone. And then, when the holidays roll around again, the magic begins anew. Of course, it never really ended, but there is just something that defies description when your feet again sink in the warm sand, you shade your eyes and scan the beach. As soon as you arrive, you go to the beach. It's what you do. Someone in the group is always there, then you sit down next to them and start a conversation that feels like you just talked with them there, in this place, yesterday, not a year ago. Time may gray the heads, grow up the members and add more people, but it doesn't impact this timeless family. Except for the added members and events, new traditions and new conversations, this family, in this place, always feels like time stands still.

Why are these people so committed to these family times and these multi-generational relationships? Because the benefits far outweigh any work, or any expense, or any perceived or real obstacle. The members of this group, which continues to grow and evolve over the years and generations, have learned a valuable lesson. Sid Taylor put it this way, *"Wisdom is perishable. Unlike information or knowledge, it cannot be stored in a computer or recorded in a book. It expires with each passing generation."* Unless we tap and enjoy that wisdom while it still thrives, it is lost to us forever. Every individual in this patchwork of friends and family has access to the wisdom of the generations, above, across and below them. That wisdom can enrich our lives beyond what we could ever read in a book, or search out on the Internet. And that is well worth desiring, and well worth a bit of commitment. If you did a survey and asked each and every person in this amazing family what this group means to them, you would hear the same word – *everything*.

How long will this family last? How long will the annual Jack's Birthday celebration continue? No one knows, but no one could have imagined it becoming what it is today, and no one can imagine it ever ending. It could very well be going strong another 25 years from now, with new families and new generations. Perhaps one day those celebrating Jack's birthday will know him only by legend. *Why, in my day...*

Granted, this private stretch of 1650 acres adjacent to the Atlantic Ocean, with 20 miles of tree-lined streets, resort amenities, three miles of beautiful sandy beaches and three championship golf courses would be, and is, a natural attraction for families and multi-generational relationships. And while these attractions are a bonus, the kinds of relationships made in this place can be created, shaped and nurtured to flourish anywhere. All it takes is a little patch of ground, maybe even your own backyard, a city park, a camping space, or some other place special and magical, where you and those you care about, and still unknown others, have staked out their own SOULinks territory.

Where, and how, can you grow your family?

Let a joy keep you.
Reach out your hands
And take it when it runs by.

Carl Sandburg

Extras

Meet the Family

The stories you have just read are about real people. Here's another opportunity for you to know them a little better. These are just bits and pieces of color you might find interesting.

Chapter One: Jennie and Andrew

You can visit the restaurant where Andrew works as executive sous chef: The Inn at Little Washington, Middle and Main Street, Washington, VA 22747. Website: http://www.theinnatlittlewashington.com/

Chapter Two: You and Me

The following are citations made in this chapter:

2. *UP: Pursuing Significance in Leadership and Life,* by Joan O. Wright. JOW Publishing, 2011. ISBN 978-0982550526.
3. *The Today Show,* NBC morning news television show. Archives: http://www.today.com/health/grandparents-grandkids-can-protect-each-others-mental-health-6C10898312

4. *"Strong grandparent-adult grandchild relationships reduce depression for both,"* American Sociological Association. http://www.eurekalert.org/pub_releases/2013-08/asa-sgg080613.php

5. *"Google Replacing Grandparents? Bleak New Study Says 'Yes.'"* The Huffington Post, by Shelley Emling, posted March 1, 2013. http://www.huffingtonpost.com/2013/03/01/google-replacing-grandparents-study_n_2789729.html

6. Jacob's blessing, Genesis 49:1-28

Chapter Three: Isabelle and Meg

Meg is a successful contributing writer at The Huffington Post, and has written her own children's book series *"Bea is for Business."* You can check out her books at her website: http://www.beaisforbusiness.com/

In 2015, Meg launched her own firm, *toth shop*, dedicated to writing, editing, and presence-building/public relations for entrepreneurs and emergent brands. The shop is named for her maternal great grandmother who left Hungary in the early 20th century as a teenager - in the middle of the night, all by herself - to come to America; it's that independent spirit that's infused in toth shop's work which is, again, one of those spirit and personality touches that Meg knows she learned to appreciate young from Isabelle. Also, on a mentoring note, Meg hires several contractor employees and many of them are former students of hers who have since graduated from college and are out in the working world, building their own personal brands and careers.

Chapter Five: Harry Chapin and Bob

Bob has over 30 years of leadership development and executive coaching experience, and is founder of LEADERSEARCH Executive Coaching Group. He loves working with executives and leaders who are moving from success to significance, or from striving to thriving. You can find out more about Bob and his work and company at the website: http://www.leadersearch.com/

Chapter Six: GranGran and Shannon

Shortly after the draft of this book was written, Shannon wrote from England where she was currently studying at Regents University in Regents Park. She said it was just a five minute walk from there to GranGran and Granddaddy's home when he was working for Xerox in the UK. They moved their family there at that time. Shannon said it was so much fun seeing the places they described, and being so close to them in memories. During that time Shannon was so happy she was able to teach that side of her family how to do FaceTime on the iPhone. Technology marches on.

Chapter Seven: Charles, Barbara and Coffee Beans

Charles was a very successful businessman from North Carolina who met Dr. Célestin Musekura of ALARM *(African Leadership and Reconciliation Ministries)* and was offered the adventure of a lifetime in Cyimbili, Rwanda, Africa. ALARM has trained over 100,000 leaders across east and central Africa. Many of the countries they have served have experienced years of war, tribal conflicts, genocide and political turmoil. Many of these places are being rebuilt one village at a time, one coffee plantation at a time.

Célestin grew up in Cyimbili and could never forget the thriving coffee plantation that served his village so well. Today, thanks much to the efforts of people like Charles and Barbara, the plantation is thriving again.

You can read about ALARM at their website:
http://alarm-inc.org/

And, if you are a coffee drinker, premium Cyimbili Coffee is once again for sale worldwide. Visit their website at: http://www.cyimbilicoffee.com/

Chapter Eight: Dorothy and Her Court

The concept of "intergenerational" living is not new, but something that goes back to the beginning of time itself. For millennia families have lived together, the very old passing along their wisdom and experiences to the younger generations, and the younger family members assisting the old in their physical presence and support. It has only been in the past century or so that we have departed from this age old family tradition. In doing so, we have unfortunately abandoned a very rich and common sense approach to generational living, and we are just now realizing this. In order to provide the best care to seniors, especially those who are dealing with health and memory issues, some have re-instituted inter-generational facilities where the very old have regular contact with the very young. If you are interested in more information on this, the following sites may be of assistance:

- **Providence Mount St. Vincent** in West Seattle, Washington - http://washington.providence.org/senior-care/mount-st-vincent/
- **Intergenerational Living and Health** Care in Eagan, Minnesota – http://www.iglhc.com/
- **Bridge Meadows** in Portland, Oregon - http://www.bridgemeadows.org/intergenerational-living/
- **Article and Video**: https://au.news.yahoo.com/sunday-night/features/a/28767461/what-happens-when-you-mix-a-nursing-home-with-childcare/
- **Article**: http://www.retirement-living.com/category/intergenerational/
- **Article**: http://extension.psu.edu/youth/intergenerational/news
- **Article**: http://www.huffingtonpost.com/susan-blumenthal/post_8756_b_6315082.html
- **Website:** http://tandf.msgfocus.com/q/1IE02XV6z6oVKJtV0WaD4/wv The Journal of Intergenerational Relationships
- **Website:** http://gu.org/HOME.aspx Generations United

Chapter Ten: Jack's Birthday and...

I provided some interesting color regarding the magical place where this amazing tradition happens each year. John's Island is truly remarkable. If you would like a little more information, visit the Club's website http://www.johnsislandclub.org/club/scripts/section/section.asp?NS=HP. You just might start your own multi-generational tradition.

SOULinks "How To" Quick Tips

Basics for Building Multi-Generational Relationships Linked at the Soul

To help remember these points, each word is a verb, an action word, and begins with each letter of **SOULINKS.** These are things we must DO, not just know.

S = SHARE

This isn't about sharing stuff, but sharing *self.* Be open and available to share of yourself, and willing to receive what your SOULink shares with you. Sharing is a two-way form of communication. Share and receive without censorship.

O = OBSERVE

Pay attention to the other person. Observe everything about this special person. Get to know him or her through careful observation of what they say, how they act, what they do. Observe in order to take advantage of any opportunity that presents itself for a better relationship, more conversation, and any chance to deepen and bless the relationship.

U = UPHOLD

Keep any agreements (do what you say you will do) made with this person, most especially upholding the bond of confidentiality. What happens between you, stays between you, and make sure your word is trustworthy.

L = LISTEN

Too often in our zeal to share or form meaningful relationships we skip this critical component by talking or doing too much and not allowing the other person the gift of our time and attention. Listen carefully to everything that is said, and even for what is not said. This is one of the greatest gifts, and rich relationship boosters, you can give another person. It's also the only way you can really *know* someone.

I = INVITE

Through words and actions, invite the other person into this relationship. Invitations come in the form of interests and identifying common ground, conversation points, and places where you can come together physically, spiritually, emotionally, intellectually and every other way. Invitations can be given through interested questions designed to know the other person better. Draw them in.

N = NURTURE

Any relationship requires work, especially nurturing. Nurturing includes tender care and encouragement for personal growth. Be aware of the other person's needs and attempt to be the inspiration, support, resource or partner he or she needs to move forward. This nurturing is necessary both in the other person, and in the relationship itself.

K = KINDLE

Kindle means to ignite interest, to encourage, promote and awaken something or someone. The easiest way to do this is to KEEP TALKING! Find the places of mutual blessing in this relationship and kindle a fire there.

S = STAND

Stand *with*, stand *by* and stand *for* the other person. This often requires unconditional love and acceptance, even in the difficult times. Stand with and stand by your SOULink through good times and bad times. Stand for, become an advocate, of the other person. This does not mean to accept and promote bad choices or behaviors. It means to continue supporting and loving the person, if not the behavior.

S	SHARE	Be open and available, share self, no censorship
O	OBSERVE	Pay attention, know through observation
U	UPHOLD	Keep agreements (confidentiality, etc.) be trustworthy
L	LISTEN	Listen carefully with heart, HEAR to know
I	INVITE	Invite into relationship, identify common ground
N	NURTURE	Foster, nurture, provide tender care *(person and relationship)*
K	KINDLE	Ignite interest, kindle fire, awaken spark
S	STAND	Stand with, stand by, and stand for

Getting Started

The best way to begin, promote and maintain any relationship is through conversation. Obviously it is best done in person, face-to-face. We learn the most about people when we can see them in person and look them in the eye. In this day of far-flung relations and high technology, however, we may have to resort to social media or other forms of communication. These are good in those times we can't be together, but they should not replace the valuable moments of shared presence.

Meaningful conversations often begin with simple questions. As opportunities arise, ask those questions that are gentle, crafted to show interest, and designed to help you understand and know your SOULink better. Start small and listen well, but don't pry and don't become a private investigator. Build a platform for the relationship to stand on, a place of mutual trust. Plan moments (events, meetings, or even conversations) of mutual benefit. Look for big moments, crossroads in either of your lives where conversation can deepen the relationship. Don't try so hard so that the other person feels uncomfortable with your probing. You want to know others better, not send them running from you.

Starter Tips

1. In order to create a SOULink, the first step is to identify the one person (or several persons) you wish to build a meaningful relationship with. Is that person an adult grandchild, a grandparent? An older or younger neighbor, or other special person in your life?

2. Consider each of the eight SOULINKS pointers above. Can you state one practical and actionable thing you could do for each one, with this person? Remember, start small and build.

3. What questions could you ask your SOULink now that would not only show your interest in that person, but would also enable you to know him or her better? *(Hobbies, special interests, sports, talents, experiences... anything.)*

4. What personal stories could you tell this person that would interest and enrich him or her, and also help to bond you two at the "soul" level?

5. How can you bless this SOULink? What can you offer him or her? *(This isn't about money or gifts. It is about a meaningful relationship.)*

And one more tip...

I wouldn't be doing my job as an executive coach without giving you a professional assessment tool that just might help in your pursuits of multi-generational relationships. Consider taking the Kolbe A ™ Index assessment. Kolbe provides materials, insights, and experts to help people of all ages identify their instinctive talents, develop their confidence, and use their innate abilities to succeed in a number of situations, from parenting, to getting through school and running a business. The Kolbe A Index is the only validated assessment that measures a person's conative strengths. Not just another personality test, Kolbe helps you understand the talent you were born with and how to Be Your Best Self. Visit http://www.kolbe.com/why-kolbe/ for more information.

There is a modest fee for this index, but well worth the rich information you can gain about yourself.

The Gift of UBUNTU

All of these pointers and beginning steps are designed to be applied by either the older or the younger member of a SOULink relationship. Either member will have unique and meaningful things to share. Those "things" will be somewhat different, due largely to age, experience and knowledge, but all are mutually beneficial. Perhaps the biggest gift you can give, the greatest motivator for relationship success, is something I learned in my travels and work in Africa. There is a saying there, used to greet people. "UBUNTU" essentially means *"I see you. I feel seen by you."* Think about that. What better gift can we give others than to truly see them, clear through to the soul, and then in return to know we are seen by them as well. Keep this in mind as you pursue these SOULink relationships, whether you are the younger, or the elder partner. What is the first thing you will do?

What can you do today,
to begin building this special
lifetime soul connection?

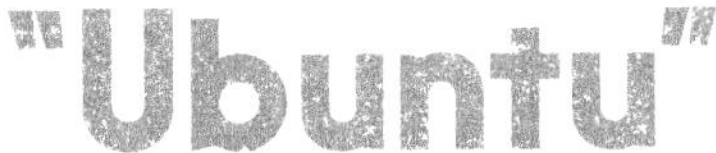

Canine Connections

As a lifelong dog person, I wanted to add this little piece under the "Extras" section because it relates to one of the best "tools" for starting a relationship – dogs. A dog has the ability to stop people in their tracks, gain their attention, and drain away tension. Conversation naturally flows in the company of dogs.

Mollie, our "senior" Jack Russell Terrier, and Duncan, our newest canine member of the family (a Cavalier King Charles Spaniel, barely out of puppy-hood) are generations apart. Although it might appear at times that Mollie really wasn't too excited about her mentor role with Duncan, she has been a faithful friend and guide for this new bundle of energy. Mollie and Duncan are pictured on the back cover of this book, in one of their rare quiet moments. Mollie has been Duncan's Yoda in the doggie kingdom. Even among animals (although some might argue dogs are more human than canine) the concept of multi-generational relationships is at work, perhaps even more so than with their human counterparts. Animals seem to have an instinctual response and understanding of their roles in multi-generational communities and situations.

Dogs not only have the ability to relate to each other in cross-generational situations, but they also have what I think is a divinely appointed skill in facilitating human-to-human relationships. There is nothing quite like a dog to bring us two-legged creatures into an instant relationship, regardless of generations. Dogs have a way of slowing us down, jump starting conversations, and comforting. They love unconditionally and are often natural comedians. They relieve anxiety and they make us smile. And smiling together over a dog can lead to beautiful relationships.

Duncan (left) and Mollie Multi-generational pals

There is a great deal of research out there about how dogs can comfort others, relieving anxiety and opening doors for healing. There is even an entire category of service and training that qualifies them to bear the title "Comfort Dog." These dogs have changed the lives of thousands, including traumatized veterans and abused children. I especially loved hearing that many courthouses around the nation are now using comfort dogs in the courtroom, for both adults and children who must provide testimony in stressful legal proceedings. With the comforting presence of a dog who knows to stay by the person's side without moving away, many have been able to get through these anxious times when they would not be able to do so any other way. There are also remarkable stories about Alzheimer's patients who have not spoken a word in years, yet will pet, greet, and speak to a dog. Scientific studies have found that the company of dogs can actually calm our central nervous systems. We aren't able to fully identify these canine connections, but we can certainly appreciate and utilize them for good.

Some dogs, regardless of pedigree, seem gifted in the smile-generating category. Both Mollie and Duncan can do that, Mollie because of her typical Jack Russell energy and comedic looks and actions, and Duncan because he looks like a little teddy bear that needs to be hugged and loved. We live next to a city park, where I walk the dogs almost daily. We can't pass someone without them smiling, making comment, or desiring to effuse over Mollie and Duncan. Sometimes it's difficult to get the walk in for exercise reasons. The walk becomes a social time instead. As Duncan got a bit older, I watched his unique behavior with others – dogs or people. He seemed to have a sense about others, what they needed from him to invite a connection. When greeting bigger dogs, he would instantly get down low, as if to acknowledge he knows he is not the alpha dog here. He does the same thing with young children, goes down as low as he can go and waits for them to come to him. He invites their company without any risk to them.

I was in the process of writing this book when I began noticing Duncan's interesting behavior with others. We were doing puppy training, but this wasn't something we taught Duncan. He did this on his own. I began paying more attention to his unique skills with others, people and canines. And I also began having more dialogue and opportunities for relationships because of Duncan. All these pieces were floating around in my head until they solidified into one concrete thought – Duncan is the ideal connection point for any relationship (including multi-generational), and, because of his inherent ability to make others feel comfortable, would make an ideal therapy dog. What a great and unique opportunity to put the concepts of my book to work in cultivating more of my own multi-generational relationships, and bringing joy to others (and Duncan and me) in the process.

I contacted Therapy Dogs International (TDI) to begin the process of training Duncan to become a therapy dog. Duncan kept showing promise, and we kept training. I joined a community of dog owners who were also getting their dogs certified. After months of intense training, the time came for Duncan's big test. And when I say "big" test, that's exactly what I mean. The training is intense, and so is the testing. I was worried about his test day, thinking I hadn't practiced enough for him to successfully pass all twelve of the "stations" where Duncan would be tested. But my faith in Duncan's abilities and unique giftedness were not misplaced. In order to become certified as a therapy dog, the dog must pass all these stations. None can be failed. To my surprise and delight, Duncan passed with flying colors. He is now certified as a therapy dog. While I doubted my own abilities and commitments to his training because of my busy schedule, I should never have doubted his "calling" into this noble profession. One woman with years of experience in dog training told me later she had her eye on Duncan from the beginning, recognizing his unique abilities as a comfort dog. She said it was so nice to see someone use those gifts in therapy, rather than showing a dog of Duncan's obvious pedigree.

Not every dog must be a certified therapy dog to be a natural connection point for relationships. Dogs just seem to be naturals that way.

I live right across the street from a Children's Cancer Center, a children's hospital and nearby assisted living facilities. We are located in the perfect place to use Duncan's ability and training to comfort others. I am currently working on establishing a connection with these places, but with Duncan, that won't be difficult. I should mention here that I first became aware of therapy dogs when a few years back our daughter, Emma Kate, was diagnosed with sarcoma, and became a patient at the Children's Cancer Center. She was visited by a therapy dog there, who lightened the otherwise stressful environment of this frightening illness. I am thrilled to say that Emma Kate is now completely healed and pursuing her PhD, and Duncan is now also a degreed canine with many comforting relationships in his future – and mine.

Not every dog must be a certified therapy dog to be a natural connection point for relationships. Dogs just seem to be naturals that way. If you are looking for a way to begin a multi-generational relationship, or any relationship, just take your dog for a walk in the park. Dogs are magnets for other like-minded *(make that "dog"-minded)* people, of any age. Don't have a dog? Go for that walk in the park anyway. Parks are full of people, full of potential relationships. Be that person who stops, looks up, and begins a conversation, wherever you are. You may change lives – *your own included.*

Want to know more about Therapy Dogs?

If you are interested in more information about therapy dogs, visit the Therapy Dogs International website: http://tdi-dog.org/

For more information about dogs used in courtrooms, see http://courthousedogs.com/

Final Thoughts...

Everything is Waiting for You

Your great mistake is to act the drama
as if you were alone. As if life
were a progressive and cunning crime
with no witness to the tiny hidden
transgressions. To feel abandoned is to deny
the intimacy of your surroundings. Surely,
even you, at times, have felt the grand array;
the swelling presence, and the chorus, crowding
out your solo voice. You must note
the way the soap dish enables you,
or the window latch grants you freedom.
Alertness is the hidden discipline of familiarity.
The stairs are your mentor of things
to come, the doors have always been there
to frighten you and invite you,
and the tiny speaker in the phone
is your dream-ladder to divinity.

Put down the weight of your aloneness and ease into
the conversation. The kettle is singing
even as it pours you a drink, the cooking pots
have left their arrogant aloofness and
seen the good in you at last. All the birds
and creatures of the world are unutterably
themselves. Everything is waiting for you.

David Whyte
from Everything is Waiting for You

"Where all of those edges meet,
you get an astonishing conversation...
an astonishing depth and
plethora of life."

David Whyte

David Whyte is a modern day poet known around the world for connecting us to ourselves and each other through his work. As you explore your own SOULinks relationships, what are the edges that need to be explored, and what new conversations can you begin?

Wishing you much joy in the pursuit.

With love,

Joanie

Joan O. Wright MSW, MCC

Joan Wright's passion for leading with significance is exemplified in her everyday living both with her family and her work with corporate leaders on four continents. She is committed to the belief that living by example and self-leadership are critical to impacting real and significant change in the world. As founder and president of O'Sullivan Wright, a global firm specializing in coaching, leadership development and talent management strategies, she is a nationally recognized Master Certified Coach and frequently sought as a speaker on leadership and change. Her nationally acclaimed book, *UP: Pursuing Significance in Leadership and Life,* inspired her to lead with significance in support of Senai Global's Climb (summiting Mount Kilimanjaro) for a Purpose. Joan also serves as a guest blogger on mariashriver.com and is among Shriver's Architect of Change Guides. Additionally, she is a coach to TEDFellows and chairs a Vistage CEO Peer Advisory Group.

Joan would love to hear your stories of multi-generational relationships. You may contact her at:

Joan@osullivanwright.com
www.osullivanwright.com
www.uppursuingsignificance.com

CPSIA information can be obtained at www.ICGtesting.com
Printed in the USA
BVOW08*1931130316

440141BV00001B/1/P

9 780982 550540